HORSE RACING
THE STATISTICAL ROUTE

WHAT ARE THE BEST STATISTICS?

WHAT ARE THE BEST PERCENTAGES FOR HORSES THAT WIN?

WHERE IS THE PROFIT OR LOSS?

STATISTICS AND ANALYSIS THAT PROVIDE THE ANSWERS
PROVIDES A DIFFERENT WAY OF LOOKING AT FORM

This book provides a valuable insight into which horses win and just as importantly, which ones lose. In all, 1374 races have been analysed by computer in a unique way, not by the actual best last place form or best average form but, best last place form and best average form in relation to other horses in the race. Also full analysis on days since last run, course winners, distance winners, top trainers, weight, top jockey and ratings. Plus, 566 of the 1374 races have been analysed to show profit and loss margins. The information is displayed in easy to follow tables and should not only be of interest to gamblers but, bookmakers, trainers, jockeys owners etc; in fact anybody with an interest in horse racing. The races have been divided into race types such as handicap hurdles, non handicap hurdles, handicap all weather etc. These groups have further been subdivided into 2 groups of runners i.e. 4-11 runners or 12+ runners, 16 groups in all. As a means of reading and really understanding the form of race horses this book will be invaluable.

Compiled by Mark Gaster

FIRST PUBLISHED 2010

©COPYRIGHT MARK GASTER

ABOUT THE BOOK and SOME HISTORY

I first started to gather information on horse races about six years ago. I guess like a lot of other people, I was looking for an edge so as to make some money. I devised a computer program that sorted the form of horses not, just into the detail but, into the best last form for the race and the best rated horse etc. On and off over the last six years I sat down and typed a lot of form from races into a computer; recording the results and saving the information as I went along and I ended up with all the details of 1374 races. For a long while I did not enter the odds of the horses in the results which were a shame but, at the time I was just looking for the type of horses that won races. That's why there is less data for profit/loss; in fact 566 races. However, I feel there is still enough data to make the profit/loss statistics relevant in most cases. Please consider that at the time I was not thinking of publishing a book to show the results but, I believe there is enough data in the profit/loss tables to make it interesting.

The problem with computer programs in relation to horse racing is that it takes a lot of time and effort to type in the races. To do a full days selection of 20+ races could take 2-3 hours and then there was still no guarantee that any program devised was going to work. A bet for most people entails sitting in the bookmakers for a half hour and then leaving after placing a few bets. Still not good if they lose but, even worse if you have just spent 2-3 hours bashing away at a keyboard. However, the programs devised would pick more winners than I ever could left to my own devices. The problem is that the bookies have had at least a couple of hundred years to get their sums right and they have done a very good job. A statistic I often hear is that 33% of all favourites win but, at average odds of 6/4 that's not enough to make a profit. Like I said they know what they are doing. Accumulators are most peoples answer but, the thing I most often hear in any bookmakers is "I had 2 or three winners but one let me down" or "I had one winner but, nothing to go with it". A 33% win rate is not going to give you many 4 out of 4 winners very often unless you are very lucky. I cannot provide you with a guaranteed 100% success rate. There is not one in the book but, I can show which horses have the highest success rate and which horses show a profit/loss according to honest statistics.

THE THING ABOUT STATISTICS

A lot of people mistrust statistics. Personally, I don't think statistics are a bad thing; it's just that statiscians often don't tell you all of the facts. For example how often do you see £250 profit made last month by Joe Bloggs, the greatest tipster in the world! What they don't tell you is that may have been the first profit made in 4 months; nothing illegal, nothing dishonest; just plain misleading. Further, they probably have that down to £100 level stakes. How many people can afford to bet on every tip given by a tipster at that rate especially if they are tipping every race. Even if it was one race a day that's £3,000 a month; £60,000 a month approx if they tip every race and imagine you just happened to pick a bad month to start following a particular tipster. **All the profit/loss margins in this book are to a £1 level stake.** I leave nothing out in the statistics and they are shown as they come. I am not going to advise you as to where to invest your money; that's a decision for you to make. My job is to show the statistics as I found them, honestly and without any bias. I am not a tipster and I do not consider that to be my job. I am sorry if that appears to be a cop out but, it is important that you understand I have no influence on the results given in this book. I am just the compiler/recorder of the facts. If I had titled this book "A Sure-fire Way to Make a Profit" then I may have felt obliged to hide some statistics or be clever in how I worded things; I am not that clever and I usually come unstuck if I try to be. So, I decided to just provide the statistics straight and let the book sell or not sell on its own merits. And anyway, how often have you seen titles like the one above; bet you've seen it all before and straight away you know the author is under pressure to prove a statistic and sell books. I am an honest person and I don't want to mislead anybody or allow anybody to misunderstand anything in this book. Take this statistic for instance that you will find later in the book:-

race type	category	position	%	num	profit/loss	num
NH-4-11	rat	1	75.63	119	-22.31	58

This shows that 75.63% of top rated horses for non handicap hurdles between 4-11 runners are placed i.e. 1st 2nd or 3rd and this is taken from 119 examples. Now, that looks pretty impressive on the surface and I could have left it at that. However, I have included the fact that from 58 of those races there is a loss of £22.31 to a £1 level stake; not so good now is it.

I would just like to make one other very important point about statistics; they are not a guarantee of what's going to happen in the future. I would love to make that guarantee but, I cannot. Statistics are a lesson in history and sometimes history repeats itself and sometimes it doesn't. You may well ask what's the point of the book then? Well I believe that if the parameters of a statistic stay the same, then there is a very good chance that the statistic will repeat itself. It is an uncertain premise with horse racing because there is always going to be factors that cannot be taken into account so, there can be no guarantees.

That's why I leave it up to you as to how you want to use this book, it's your money, it's your decision and it must be that way. I do not give advice on this however, the information provided has taken a lot of work and time to collate and I believe there is a lot to learn from it and it should help you with whatever strategies you have. It is with this in mind that I believe the book will prove very helpful otherwise; I would not have published the book.

Please Read Through The Next Section Carefully As It Is Very Important That You Understand Fully How The Data Has Been Collected And Sorted.

HOW THE DATA WAS COLLECTED AND STORED

Excel worksheet in Microsoft was used to enter and sort the details and runners of each race. The details of each race were entered in this way:-

Race type (handicap hurdle, non handicap hurdle, handicap chase, flat etc)
Distance of race
Going of race
Class of race
Number of runners

The following details of each horse in each race were also entered:-

Place figure for last race run
Average of the last three place figures
Days since last run
Course winner
Distance winner
Top trainer for the course
Weight
Top jockey for the course
Rating

When I first started to collect the information I came to realise that a horse that came 4th in its last race could be very good placing or not in relation to other horses in the race. To explain – If a horse came 4th in its last race and all of the other horses in the race came 1st, 2nd or 3rd then a 4th place doesn't read very well. However, if every other horse in the race came 5th, 6th, 7th etc then a 4th place takes on a different meaning and reads very well in the context of that race. I felt this was an important consideration so; I developed a program to take that into account, by sorting the last place figure for each horse into best last place, second best last place and so on.

Let me demonstrate that - imagine the following table as representing the last three place figures (in bold) of the horses in a six horse race:-

horse num	place1	place2	**place3**
1	4	5	**8**
2	1	2	**2**
3	1	2	**4**
4	5	5	**6**
5	7	7	**5**
6	9	9	**3**

The table shows that in the fourth column 2nd is the best place figure, 3rd the second best figure and so on. The program transformed these figures so that horse number one would have the 6th best form figure, horse number two would have the 1st best form figure and horse number three would have the 3rd best figure and so on. Now the same table above would read like this.

horse num	place1	place2	**place3**
1	4	5	**6**
2	1	2	**1**
3	1	2	**3**
4	5	5	**5**
5	7	7	**4**
6	9	9	**2**

Nearly all of the forms of horses have been treated in this way. Lets expand that table and take the average of the last three place figures for the same 6 horse race; they are as follows:-

horse	place1	place2	place3	**average of last 3 place figures**
1	4	5	8	**5.67**
2	1	2	2	**1.67**
3	1	2	4	**2.33**
4	5	5	6	**5.33**
5	7	7	5	**6.33**
6	9	9	3	**7.00**

Again these were sorted into the best average, second best average and so on. Horse number one has the 4th best average; horse number two has the 1st best average and so on. Therefore, the column for average of last three figures would now look like this:-

horse	place1	place2	place3	average of last 3 place figures
1	4	5	8	2
2	1	2	2	3
3	1	2	4	4
4	5	5	6	1
5	7	7	5	5
6	9	9	3	6

As well as the last place figure and average last three place figures - days, weight and ratings were treated in the same way. Course winners, distance winners, top trainers for the course, and top jockeys for the course were just simply marked with a 1; no sorting necessary. I will deal with days, weight and ratings in more detail later but, first let me show you a full entry as I typed it out and then how that information looked after being sorted:-

horse num	place1	place2	place3	days	course	dist	trainer	weight	jockey	rating
1	4	5	8	35	1	1	1	96	0	77
2	1	2	2	20	0	1	1	810	0	75
3	1	2	4	5	0	0	0	89	1	78
4	5	5	6	25	0	0	0	85	0	65
5	7	7	5	121	0	0	0	710	1	62
6	9	9	3	11	0	1	0	76	0	55

The above is an example of the information as typed from the newspapers; every race was entered in this way. The following table shows that information after it had been sorted:-

horse num	last placing	average	days	course	dist	trainer	weight	jockey	rating
1	6	3	4	1	1	1	4	0	2
2	1	1	3	0	1	1	3	0	3
3	3	1	1	0	0	0	3	1	1
4	5	2	3	0	0	0	2	0	4
5	4	3	5	0	0	0	1	1	5
6	2	4	2	0	1	0	0	0	6

As you can see this puts a different perspective on the "form" but, I think a better way of reading a race especially for analysing statistics. An extra column has been added for the average and the first two place columns have been ditched. All of the information in this book shows the results from tables that have been sorted in this way. For instance – taking an example from the book the following table shows that the best averaged horses of NFL races of between 4-11 runners win 19.02% of the time (second row). **This does not mean horses that had an average of 1 but, horses that had**

the best average of all the horses in those races. Sorry to keep making the point but, it is important that you understand this.

race type	category	position	%	num	profit/loss	num
NFL-4-11	rat	1	29.37	126	-6.51	43
NFL-4-11	ave	1	19.02	184	-11.81	58
NFL-4-11	rat	2	18.75	160	-14.25	54
NFL-4-11	cou	1	18.18	88	-10.90	29

I realise this will be confusing but, to get the proper use of the data in this book it is important to get used to this. It is not as difficult as it seems once you do, after all, this is what gives the book its unique perspective on reading the form. I have not come across other programs or, books that have done this; there may be one somewhere but, I have not found one to date. Yet, I believe it is important to _see_ the form in this way, I could have provided you with a lot of statistics that showed the results of all the horses that came 4th last time out in particular races but, is that relevant? Showing you the statistics for all of the horses that had the 4th best last form I think is far more relevant; I hope you agree.

The following section provides more detail of how the tables are presented and their meaning, please read through carefully.

FURTHER EXPLANATION of TABLES

An example of the first two lines of a table

race type	category	position	%	num	profit/loss	num
HH-4-11	rat	1	22.94	109	-17.32	57

Please Note :-(there is a full list of abbreviations later in the book)

Race type
Each table is headed as above. The first column indicates race type which is represented by type and number of runners. The following abbreviations are used for race types:-
HH-handicap hurdles
NH non handicap hurdles
HCH- handicap chases
NCH- non handicap chases
HAW- handicap all weather
NAW-non handicap all weather
HFL-handicap flat
NFL-non handicap flat

These are further divided into two by number of runners i.e. 4-11 runners or 12+ runners. So, in the example in the table above, HH-4-11 denotes Handicap Hurdles of 4-11 runners.

Category

Indicates the type of form in question; there are nine categories, (abbreviations in brackets)

Last place form	(pla)
Average of last three form figures	(ave)
Days since last win	(day)
Course winners	(cou)
Distance winners	(dis)
Top trainer for course	(tra)
Weight	(wei)
Top jockey for course	(joc)
Ratings	(rat)

Position.

Denotes the position of the category in question so, rat with a 1 in the next column, and denotes horses that had the best rating for the type of races in question or ave with a 3 in the next column denotes horses that had the third best average and so on.

Percentage or %

Shows the percentage results of the analysis.

Number shown as num

The amount of examples found in the data for that particular race type and category/position. In the example above 109 examples of rat 1 were found and analysed for HH-4-11 i.e. handicap hurdles with 4-11 runners.

Profit/loss

Shows the amount of profit or loss for that category/position to a £1 level stake. In the case above it shows that rat 1 showed a loss (-) of £17.32

Number shown as num

Again, shows the amount of examples found in the data for that particular race type and category/position. In the case above 57 examples were analysed for profit/loss.

FURTHER DETAIL ABOUT CATOGARIES-POSITION

Place(pla) - Pretty much covered this but, just to reiterate place 1 and place 2 denotes best place and second best place not, actual as in came first last time out or second last time out etc.

Average(ave) – Again same as in place but, its worth mentioning that if there was only one or two figures to go on then 5 was substituted for a blank place. For example the form figures for a horse might read 45 or just 4 as they had only had one or two runs. To work out the average in each case 545 or 554 was calculated.

IMPORTANT POINT- the average does not have to worked in practice; just by adding the form figures together will give the same result. For example two horses with form figures 222 and 444 added together you get 6 and 12 which will still show that the first horse has the best average and the second horse has the second best average. When you're looking through horse form in a newspaper and you want to see which horse has the third best average for instance; then it is far easier to do it this way, by just adding the figures- it will provide the same answer. This is a lot easier than trying to work out all of the actual averages.

Days (day) – denotes the figure given in most newspapers for the amount of days since the horse last ran. For the purpose of this each horse was put into a group of 1-10 days, 11-20 days, 21-30 days, and so on; all horses over 100 days since last run were lumped together. So, in the tables a category marked - day 2 - for example; denotes horses that were second fittest in relation to other horse. But, bear in mind if you are studying form all horses that are marked between 21 and 30 days for example will be given the same position. This appears a bit complicated so, to explain it further look at the following table:-

horse number	days since last run	position after sorting
1	15	1
2	19	1
3	25	2
4	42	3
5	46	3
6	54	4

As you can see horses 1 and 2 end up with the same position and the same goes for horses 4 and 5. However, don't worry too much as days do not feature very much in the tables. Just remember that positions 1 to 10 means fittest, second fittest and so on.

Course winners (cou), Distance winners (dis) – No need for much sorting here; course winners/distance winners were marked with a 1. Joint course and distance winners were not dealt with but, later in the book I have put some statistics for profit/loss for course **and** distance winners.

Top Trainers (tra)/Top Jockeys (joc) – Most newspapers give a list of top trainers and top jockeys for each course. When this data was being compiled any trainer listed in the top trainers list was marked with a 1, irrespective of where it came in the list; the same applied to top jockey lists.

Weight (wei) – This is a bit more complicated and the weights were sorted into nine groups; the following table explains those groups:-

weight range	allocated number
7-0 - 7-13	1
8-0 - 8-6	2
8-7 - 8-13	3
9-0 - 9-6	4
9-7 - 9-13	5
10-0 - 10-6	6
10-7 - 10-13	7
11-0 - 11-6	8
11-7+	9

As you can see each group is numbered so, in the program each horse was accorded the respective number according to their weight. To make things more complicated they were further sorted into best, second best, third best and so on, starting with the lowest weights first. Therefore when you see "wei 1" in the tables this means the lowest group of weights, "wei 4" means the highest weights in the race; "wei 2" or "wei 3" is the lower middle and the higher middle respectively. In handicaps there are more weight differences and sometimes there could be up to 5 different groups but this was quite rare. Just to help make this clearer, look at the following table:-

horse number	weight	figure accorded each horse	position after sorting
1	11-10	9	4
2	11-3	8	3
3	10-9	7	2
4	10-8	7	2
5	10-5	6	1
6	10-4	6	1

In this book all the analysis was based on figures derived from examples of the last column i.e. position after sorting.

Rating (rat) – Ratings are given in most daily newspapers. There is always one top rated horse that is usually highlighted by a black spot and the other horses would be accorded a figure below that. For example, the ratings in the Daily Mail which were used for this book give the top rated horse as 78 and thereafter other horses could be rated 76, 75, and 74, and so on down to 40. More than one horse could be rated 77 or 74 say. Again for the purpose of this book they were rated according to best, second best and so on irrespective of the actual rating.

SUMMARY on HOW TO READ THE TABLES

I appreciate that the above makes things appear complicated but, in practice once you get used to reading the form in this way it's not so difficult. Certainly once you start looking at the tables in the book it will become a lot clearer. I have had to explain everything carefully but, in practise it will not be necessary to calculate everything in all of the tables. Mostly, it is last place form 1, 2, 3, average form 1, 2, 3 and ratings 1, 2, 3 that will become relevant when using the tables.

On balance, I think the way the form has been sorted and presented is a better way of reading a race than just taking the form as literal. In the context of a horse race I think it is far more relevant knowing which horse has the best last place form than just knowing its last place form was 4th. Certainly, for obtaining statistics that are relevant and presenting those to you in this way will prove more useful than just reading bare form.

NOTE: - In nearly all of the tables in this book only the first 18 results have been shown. This was to save space and make the book more compact. The column that's relevant to the table's title has been highlighted in bold. Also, if less than 10 examples of any particular statistic were found the results have not been included in the tables, where this occurs the appropriate result has been marked n/a (non applicable). Two tables have been omitted altogether for this reason; they are the profit/loss tables for non-handicap chases of 12+ runners and non-handicap all weather races of 12+ runners. National flat races, nurseries and claimers were not analysed at all.

The book has been divided into four main sections:–

WIN ONLY PERCENTAGE: - results obtained for horses that have won races only.
PLACE ONLY PERCENTAGE: - results obtained for horses that have won or been placed in their races.
WIN ONLY PROFIT/LOSS: - results showing the profit loss to a £1 stake to bookmakers returned odds for horses that won their races only.
PLACE ONLY PROFIT/LOSS: - results showing the profit loss to a £1 E/W stake to bookmakers returned odds for horses that won or were placed in their races. Calculated to include 1/4 odds for certain races and 1/5 odds for others.
PLACE ONLY WITHOUT WIN ODDS: - A single table dealing with profit/loss for place only odds.
FURTHER TABLES DEALING WITH: - course, distance, trainer, jockeys course & distance and going.

SORTING THE WHEAT FROM THE CHAFF: - sorts all of the
information to show the best information to profit/loss.

ABBREVIATIONS USED IN THIS BOOK

pla	last place form
ave	average of last form figures
day	days since last run
cou	course winner
dis	distance winner
tra	top trainer
joc	top jockey
rat	rating
num	number
12+	12 or more runners
4-11	4-11 runners
HH	handicap hurdle
NH	non handicap hurdle
HCH	handicap chase
NCH	non handicap chase
HAW	handicap all weather
NAW	non handicap all weather
HFL	handicap flat
NFL	non handicap flat
prof/loss	profit/loss
e/w	each way
n/a	non applicable
c&d	course and distance

I hope the previous sections have made it clear the way the book has been
compiled. I apologise if I have overdone these explanations but, I think it is
important that there is no misunderstanding. Please read through again
carefully if you still are not sure but, I think once you start to read through
the following tables it will be easier to understand.

The next section begins by showing the actual statistics as computed from
the data. The main theme of each table is highlighted in bold type. The first
section that begins on the next page deals with win only percentage. That is,
only horses that have won races.

WIN ONLY PERCENTAGE

Handicap Hurdle 4-11 runners (109 Races Analysed)

race type	category	position	%	num	profit/loss	num
HH-4-11	rat	1	22.94	109	-17.32	57
HH-4-11	pla	1	19.51	164	-4.02	84
HH-4-11	ave	1	18.03	183	-27.85	93
HH-4-11	cou	1	16.85	89	17.28	46
HH-4-11	day	1	16.74	221	-11.92	121
HH-4-11	dis	1	15.38	260	-13.05	149
HH-4-11	pla	2	15.12	172	-27.40	90
HH-4-11	joc	1	13.98	186	7.80	94
HH-4-11	wei	3	13.68	285	0.53	147
HH-4-11	wei	2	12.98	285	-29.35	150
HH-4-11	ave	2	12.50	240	-5.72	114
HH-4-11	rat	3	12.04	191	-54.15	98
HH-4-11	day	3	11.67	180	-36.95	102
HH-4-11	wei	4	11.67	180	-11.97	105
HH-4-11	tra	1	11.61	155	-33.75	81
HH-4-11	day	5	10.92	119	0.00	65
HH-4-11	pla	4	10.63	160	-13.50	86
HH-4-11	rat	2	10.53	228	-35.25	112

Handicap Hurdle 12+ runners (69 Races Analysed)

race type	category	position	%	num	profit/loss	num
HH-12+	rat	1	15.94	69	-12.58	26
HH-12+	ave	1	14.14	99	3.88	36
HH-12+	rat	3	11.34	194	37.00	65
HH-12+	pla	9	10.71	28	41.00	14
HH-12+	ave	2	8.82	204	-7.70	65
HH-12+	pla	1	8.50	153	-15.13	59
HH-12+	day	3	8.50	200	-26.50	77
HH-12+	pla	3	8.45	142	-38.00	45
HH-12+	pla	2	8.39	143	-22.70	53
HH-12+	cou	1	8.33	108	-6.00	34
HH-12+	rat	2	8.12	197	-42.00	70
HH-12+	wei	2	7.84	319	14.50	103
HH-12+	dis	1	7.78	360	-8.50	108
HH-12+	wei	3	7.36	299	-45.08	103
HH-12+	wei	4	6.99	186	-22.00	86
HH-12+	pla	8	6.85	73	-24.00	24
HH-12+	day	1	6.71	164	-26.83	70
HH-12+	ave	8	6.67	15	n/a	8

WIN ONLY PERCENTAGE

Non Handicap Hurdle 4-11 runners (119 Races Analysed)

race type	category	position	%	num	profit/loss	num
NH-4-11	rat	1	35.29	119	-21.68	58
NH-4-11	cou	1	27.50	40	-4.20	17
NH-4-11	ave	1	25.40	189	3.94	93
NH-4-11	rat	2	22.22	135	6.51	67
NH-4-11	tra	1	21.08	223	2.40	88
NH-4-11	pla	1	20.39	206	-53.19	101
NH-4-11	pla	2	19.77	177	20.54	86
NH-4-11	joc	1	19.41	273	-30.52	119
NH-4-11	dis	1	17.83	129	-34.07	61
NH-4-11	wei	3	16.91	136	-41.75	52
NH-4-11	ave	2	16.84	196	38.38	89
NH-4-11	day	2	13.87	274	-35.05	144
NH-4-11	day	1	12.89	256	-8.67	128
NH-4-11	wei	2	11.23	543	-72.32	259
NH-4-11	day	4	10.59	170	-55.65	82
NH-4-11	ave	3	9.87	223	-83.62	109
NH-4-11	day	3	9.71	206	-53.94	104
NH-4-11	rat	3	9.32	161	-29.63	80

Non Handicap Hurdle 12+ runners (67 Races Analysed)

race type	category	position	%	num	profit/loss	num
NH-12+	wei	4	36.36	11	n/a	4
NH-12+	rat	1	32.84	67	-11.75	32
NH-12+	rat	2	22.08	77	-4.25	37
NH-12+	ave	1	18.70	123	-5.28	51
NH-12+	cou	1	17.65	34	-14.77	18
NH-12+	dis	1	14.29	119	-28.58	48
NH-12+	day	4	13.99	143	46.14	66
NH-12+	joc	1	13.81	181	7.19	76
NH-12+	pla	1	12.75	149	-32.06	61
NH-12+	tra	1	11.89	185	-23.81	77
NH-12+	pla	2	10.53	133	-32.24	62
NH-12+	wei	3	10.43	115	-1.37	48
NH-12+	ave	3	8.99	178	-22.25	89
NH-12+	pla	3	8.33	132	-47.63	67
NH-12+	ave	2	8.33	180	-56.40	70
NH-12+	day	3	7.55	159	-25.02	66
NH-12+	pla	4	6.82	132	3.00	63
NH-12+	day	5	6.80	103	-43.50	46

WIN ONLY PERCENTAGE

Handicap Chase 4-11 runners (153 Races Analysed)

race type	category	position	%	num	profit/loss	num
HCH-4-11	ave	1	22.22	234	-29.20	93
HCH-4-11	pla	1	21.63	245	-27.70	105
HCH-4-11	rat	1	17.65	153	-19.95	62
HCH-4-11	tra	1	17.06	252	2.38	84
HCH-4-11	cou	1	15.58	199	1.13	94
HCH-4-11	joc	1	15.55	283	12.58	105
HCH-4-11	rat	2	14.81	324	-19.13	132
HCH-4-11	wei	3	14.67	375	-2.38	149
HCH-4-11	day	1	13.73	357	-21.88	159
HCH-4-11	pla	2	13.19	235	-31.13	91
HCH-4-11	day	2	13.17	334	-63.75	147
HCH-4-11	ave	3	13.09	275	-49.25	112
HCH-4-11	dis	1	12.56	414	-67.33	191
HCH-4-11	ave	2	12.14	280	-8.38	113
HCH-4-11	wei	2	12.09	364	-51.70	157
HCH-4-11	wei	4	11.86	194	-6.04	71
HCH-4-11	pla	3	11.54	260	-14.25	101
HCH-4-11	day	5	11.54	104	-1.00	43

Handicap Chase 12+ runners (51 Races Analysed)

race type	category	position	%	num	profit/loss	num
HCH-12+	pla	2	12.73	110	20.50	45
HCH-12+	pla	8	12.00	25	n/a	8
HCH-12+	pla	1	11.59	138	3.25	59
HCH-12+	rat	5	10.99	91	9.00	35
HCH-12+	day	4	10.28	107	-7.00	42
HCH-12+	joc	1	9.86	142	-20.50	56
HCH-12+	ave	2	9.64	166	31.50	68
HCH-12+	day	8	9.52	21	n/a	5
HCH-12+	day	1	9.35	139	20.75	60
HCH-12+	ave	1	8.94	123	-11.75	40
HCH-12+	rat	3	8.40	131	-10.00	49
HCH-12+	rat	4	8.26	121	18.00	45
HCH-12+	wei	2	8.11	185	-13.00	66
HCH-12+	rat	1	7.84	51	-12.25	21
HCH-12+	wei	1	7.77	206	7.75	74
HCH-12+	rat	6	7.69	91	-22.00	43
HCH-12+	dis	1	7.03	256	-25.25	98
HCH-12+	ave	4	6.57	137	-9.00	51

WIN ONLY PERCENTAGE

Non Handicap Chase 4-11 runners (75 Races Analysed)

race type	category	position	%	num	profit/loss	num
NCH-4-11	rat	1	41.33	75	2.32	25
NCH-4-11	wei	3	38.10	21	n/a	7
NCH-4-11	ave	1	28.57	119	-15.98	42
NCH-4-11	pla	1	25.41	122	-1.57	41
NCH-4-11	dis	1	20.69	87	-3.01	28
NCH-4-11	joc	1	19.23	156	-23.82	53
NCH-4-11	tra	1	19.05	126	-11.50	39
NCH-4-11	pla	2	17.92	106	-17.00	34
NCH-4-11	ave	2	16.92	130	-21.01	43
NCH-4-11	rat	2	15.93	113	-14.00	40
NCH-4-11	day	1	15.60	141	-36.25	62
NCH-4-11	day	2	15.38	156	-19.58	54
NCH-4-11	wei	2	14.80	196	-37.40	65
NCH-4-11	day	4	14.29	70	0.25	25
NCH-4-11	day	3	13.46	104	-18.75	29
NCH-4-11	rat	3	11.71	111	-4.15	26
NCH-4-11	wei	1	11.58	311	-48.33	109
NCH-4-11	pla	3	11.30	115	-9.26	40

Non Handicap Chase 12+ runners (11 Races Analysed)

NOTE: - THIS IS A LOW NUMBER OF RACES ANALYSED

race type	category	position	%	num	profit/loss	num
NCH-12+	rat	2	26.67	15	n/a	5
NCH-12+	pla	2	23.08	26	n/a	6
NCH-12+	cou	1	20.00	15	n/a	5
NCH-12+	rat	1	18.18	11	n/a	2
NCH-12+	ave	3	14.71	34	n/a	7
NCH-12+	day	2	13.04	23	n/a	7
NCH-12+	ave	1	12.90	31	n/a	6
NCH-12+	day	3	11.43	35	n/a	4
NCH-12+	joc	1	10.81	37	n/a	6
NCH-12+	day	8	10.00	10	n/a	2
NCH-12+	pla	1	9.09	33	n/a	6
NCH-12+	dis	1	9.09	33	-10.17	12
NCH-12+	tra	1	9.09	44	4.00	11
NCH-12+	rat	3	8.70	23	n/a	3
NCH-12+	wei	1	8.16	49	n/a	3
NCH-12+	day	1	7.69	26	n/a	5

WIN ONLY PERCENTAGE

Handicap All Weather 4-11 runners (141 Races Analysed)

race type	category	position	%	num	profit/loss	num
HAW-4-11	rat	1	20.57	141	-25.78	71
HAW-4-11	pla	1	19.83	237	-16.10	120
HAW-4-11	ave	1	19.43	211	-52.23	105
HAW-4-11	wei	4	16.33	49	29.50	16
HAW-4-11	tra	1	16.23	154	-32.84	69
HAW-4-11	pla	3	13.57	199	3.38	102
HAW-4-11	day	4	13.53	170	-6.42	89
HAW-4-11	rat	2	13.40	306	-32.91	148
HAW-4-11	rat	3	13.17	319	95.50	154
HAW-4-11	day	1	12.94	340	-54.66	168
HAW-4-11	wei	3	12.71	299	-91.65	168
HAW-4-11	dis	1	12.35	688	-112.13	323
HAW-4-11	pla	2	12.18	197	-53.09	100
HAW-4-11	ave	2	12.11	256	-0.40	126
HAW-4-11	ave	3	11.88	261	-42.79	134
HAW-4-11	day	2	11.65	369	-42.46	178
HAW-4-11	wei	2	11.28	532	-87.63	264
HAW-4-11	joc	1	10.89	257	10.74	113

Handicap All Weather 12+ runners (79 Races Analysed)

race type	category	position	%	num	profit/loss	num
HAW-12+	rat	1	25.32	79	15.13	33
HAW-12+	pla	1	21.29	155	13.26	60
HAW-12+	ave	1	12.80	125	-43.13	60
HAW-12+	cou	1	12.00	325	8.13	146
HAW-12+	wei	4	11.76	17	n/a	5
HAW-12+	joc	1	11.34	194	-17.00	70
HAW-12+	ave	2	10.63	160	14.75	72
HAW-12+	day	2	10.26	312	32.88	127
HAW-12+	day	1	10.19	206	-27.88	88
HAW-12+	pla	6	9.86	142	122.00	61
HAW-12+	dis	1	9.76	461	-4.13	220
HAW-12+	rat	3	9.09	242	-18.37	96
HAW-12+	ave	7	8.77	57	-18.00	18
HAW-12+	ave	4	8.72	172	34.38	67
HAW-12+	wei	3	8.47	177	-15.50	81
HAW-12+	rat	9	7.69	13	n/a	7
HAW-12+	wei	2	7.54	491	-102.50	217

WIN ONLY PERCENTAGE

Non Handicap All Weather 4-11 runners (84 Races Analysed)

race type	category	position	%	num	profit/loss	num
NAW-4-11	rat	1	**36.90**	84	9.12	30
NAW-4-11	ave	1	**26.23**	122	-6.23	41
NAW-4-11	pla	1	**23.14**	121	-14.68	41
NAW-4-11	joc	1	**17.72**	158	-12.88	47
NAW-4-11	pla	2	**17.04**	135	-12.33	51
NAW-4-11	ave	2	**17.01**	147	5.13	57
NAW-4-11	tra	1	**17.00**	100	4.25	30
NAW-4-11	rat	2	**16.67**	96	-9.75	35
NAW-4-11	dis	1	**15.52**	116	0.75	46
NAW-4-11	wei	2	**13.51**	333	-9.92	120
NAW-4-11	day	3	**13.22**	174	-41.13	55
NAW-4-11	cou	1	**12.66**	79	1.25	33
NAW-4-11	day	2	**12.50**	200	-17.72	78
NAW-4-11	rat	3	**11.65**	103	-31.38	42
NAW-4-11	day	4	**11.57**	121	-37.50	52
NAW-4-11	pla	3	**10.13**	158	-5.50	45
NAW-4-11	wei	1	**10.06**	338	-65.58	127
NAW-4-11	day	1	**9.46**	148	9.85	51

Non Handicap All Weather 12+ runners (37 Races Analysed)

race type	category	position	%	num	profit/loss	num
NAW-12+	rat	1	**27.03**	37	n/a	8
NAW-12+	pla	1	**21.05**	57	1.00	11
NAW-12+	ave	1	**18.75**	64	5.50	14
NAW-12+	day	1	**15.46**	97	-8.25	25
NAW-12+	rat	2	**15.38**	52	n/a	9
NAW-12+	joc	1	**14.55**	110	-7.00	22
NAW-12+	pla	2	**13.43**	67	6.00	12
NAW-12+	rat	3	**12.50**	48	n/a	9
NAW-12+	pla	3	**11.48**	61	-10.25	14
NAW-12+	dis	1	**11.27**	71	-5.50	12
NAW-12+	ave	3	**10.34**	87	-11.50	16
NAW-12+	tra	1	**10.14**	69	-6.00	11
NAW-12+	day	5	**10.00**	60	-4.00	11
NAW-12+	ave	2	**9.76**	82	-8.00	16
NAW-12+	wei	2	**9.76**	164	-16.50	26
NAW-12+	wei	3	**9.52**	21	n/a	7
NAW-12+	cou	1	**8.16**	49	n/a	4
NAW-12+	wei	1	**7.01**	271	-41.75	66

WIN ONLY PERCENTAGE

Handicap Flat 4-11 runners (168 Races Analysed)

race type	category	position	%	num	profit/loss	num
HFL4-11	rat	1	21.43	168	-5.17	61
HFL4-11	ave	1	18.96	269	-29.40	96
HFL4-11	day	6	17.14	35	-1.00	10
HFL4-11	pla	1	17.12	292	-26.96	101
HFL4-11	cou	1	16.34	202	34.05	81
HFL4-11	wei	4	15.18	112	-9.50	19
HFL4-11	wei	3	14.29	413	-25.20	144
HFL4-11	day	3	13.38	284	-73.32	110
HFL4-11	pla	2	13.33	240	-34.78	88
HFL4-11	pla	5	13.30	218	29.00	77
HFL4-11	rat	2	13.26	347	8.10	131
HFL4-11	dis	1	12.88	722	-96.24	291
HFL4-11	joc	1	12.37	388	-24.06	138
HFL4-11	day	1	12.23	417	-28.95	158
HFL4-11	ave	2	11.82	296	-14.62	108
HFL4-11	rat	3	11.08	397	-48.76	148
HFL4-11	tra	1	10.88	239	-44.97	105
HFL4-11	day	2	10.66	422	-38.25	161

Handicap Flat 12+ runners (56 Races Analysed)

race type	category	position	%	num	profit/loss	num
HFL12+	wei	4	12.90	31	13.00	12
HFL12+	joc	1	12.66	158	4.00	47
HFL12+	pla	5	12.50	88	22.00	32
HFL12+	day	6	11.54	52	26.00	15
HFL12+	pla	1	10.53	95	-16.63	38
HFL12+	pla	4	9.68	93	5.50	37
HFL12+	ave	1	9.68	93	-2.88	36
HFL12+	rat	5	9.09	88	51.75	34
HFL12+	ave	2	8.97	145	-18.00	61
HFL12+	rat	1	8.93	56	-15.63	22
HFL12+	cou	1	8.77	114	-33.00	37
HFL12+	day	2	8.42	202	-36.25	64
HFL12+	rat	4	8.24	170	-14.00	53
HFL12+	tra	1	8.18	110	-26.00	40
HFL12+	rat	2	7.93	164	0.00	69
HFL12+	wei	3	7.91	215	-8.75	83
HFL12+	ave	4	7.87	127	-17.00	53
HFL12+	dis	1	7.44	390	-26.38	154

WIN ONLY PERCENTAGE

Non Handicap Flat 4-11 runners (126 Races Analysed)

race type	category	position	%	num	profit/loss	num
NFL-4-11	rat	1	29.37	126	-6.51	43
NFL-4-11	ave	1	19.02	184	-11.81	58
NFL-4-11	rat	2	18.75	160	-14.25	54
NFL-4-11	cou	1	18.18	88	-10.90	29
NFL-4-11	pla	1	17.43	218	15.78	82
NFL-4-11	ave	2	17.21	215	9.10	71
NFL-4-11	rat	3	16.15	161	26.80	55
NFL-4-11	wei	3	15.56	45	-1.00	10
NFL-4-11	joc	1	15.43	311	-46.37	79
NFL-4-11	day	4	14.77	149	-14.75	58
NFL-4-11	day	5	14.75	61	-9.70	14
NFL-4-11	wei	2	14.22	422	-20.72	116
NFL-4-11	pla	3	13.51	185	-16.75	59
NFL-4-11	tra	1	13.23	189	-41.42	66
NFL-4-11	day	1	13.03	261	-40.50	91
NFL-4-11	dis	1	12.69	260	-22.85	95
NFL-4-11	pla	2	12.14	206	-31.74	67
NFL-4-11	pla	4	11.73	179	-51.00	60

Non Handicap Flat 12+ runners (29 Races Analysed)

race type	category	position	%	num	profit/loss	num
NFL-12+	rat	1	27.59	29	2.23	15
NFL-12+	rat	6	19.44	36	21.00	15
NFL-12+	pla	1	15.25	59	7.55	36
NFL-12+	ave	2	14.10	78	-11.77	37
NFL-12+	pla	3	12.50	56	-9.37	25
NFL-12+	tra	1	12.16	74	-7.62	45
NFL-12+	ave	1	12.00	50	2.50	21
NFL-12+	dis	1	11.11	72	-4.12	41
NFL-12+	joc	1	10.89	101	-19.80	51
NFL-12+	rat	2	10.53	38	-14.30	19
NFL-12+	day	4	10.17	59	-11.70	34
NFL-12+	day	2	10.00	100	-31.30	60
NFL-12+	cou	1	10.00	20	16.00	10
NFL-12+	pla	2	9.80	51	-27.00	27
NFL-12+	wei	2	9.33	193	-36.57	86
NFL-12+	ave	3	8.57	70	-23.80	37
NFL-12+	pla	8	8.33	12	n/a	6
NFL-12+	rat	3	8.11	37	-16.25	19

WIN ONLY PERCENTAGE

Best Of all Race Types/Categories (1374 Races Analysed)

race type	category	position	%	num	profit/loss	num
NCH-4-11	rat	1	41.33	75	2.32	25
NCH-4-11	wei	3	38.10	21	n/a	7
NAW-4-11	rat	1	36.90	84	9.12	30
NH-12+	wei	4	36.36	11	n/a	4
NH-4-11	rat	1	35.29	119	-21.68	58
NH-12+	rat	1	32.84	67	-11.75	32
NFL-4-11	rat	1	29.37	126	-6.51	43
NCH-4-11	ave	1	28.57	119	-15.98	42
NFL-12+	rat	1	27.59	29	2.23	15
NH-4-11	cou	1	27.50	40	-4.20	17
NAW-12+	rat	1	27.03	37	n/a	8
NCH-12+	rat	2	26.67	15	n/a	5
NAW-4-11	ave	1	26.23	122	-6.23	41
NCH-4-11	pla	1	25.41	122	-1.57	41
NH-4-11	ave	1	25.40	189	3.94	93
HAW-12+	rat	1	25.32	79	15.13	33
NAW-4-11	pla	1	23.14	121	-14.68	41
NCH-12+	pla	2	23.08	26	n/a	6
HH-4-11	rat	1	23	109	-17	57
NH-4-11	rat	2	22.22	135	6.51	67
HCH-4-11	ave	1	22.22	234	-29.20	93
NH-12+	rat	2	22.08	77	-4.25	37
HCH-4-11	pla	1	21.63	245	-27.70	105
HFL4-11	rat	1	21.43	168	-5.17	61
HAW-12+	pla	1	21.29	155	13.26	60
NH-4-11	tra	1	21.08	223	2.40	88
NAW-12+	pla	1	21.05	57	1.00	11
NCH-4-11	dis	1	20.69	87	-3.01	28
HAW-4-11	rat	1	20.57	141	-25.78	71
NH-4-11	pla	1	20.39	206	-53.19	101
NCH-12+	cou	1	20.00	15	n/a	5
HAW-4-11	pla	1	19.83	237	-16.10	120
NH-4-11	pla	2	19.77	177	20.54	86
HH-4-11	pla	1	20	164	-4	84
NFL-12+	rat	6	19.44	36	21.00	15

PLACE ONLY PERCENTAGE

The following tables refer to horses that were placed only including a win. So, these tables only include horses that were placed 1st, 2nd or 3rd. The bookmakers do include a 4th placed horse in there payouts for some races but, these were not included in the calculations. At the time of writing these are usually only handicaps of 16 or more runners. These tables have only been based on 1st, 2nd or 3rd placeings. This should not have had a great effect on the results as not many handicaps of 16 or more runners were recorded in the database.

PLACE ONLY PERCENTAGE

Handicap Hurdle 4-11 runners (109 Races Analysed)

race type	category	position	%	num	profit/loss	num
HH-4-11	rat	1	57.80	109	-28.22	57
HH-4-11	pla	1	45.12	164	-21.77	84
HH-4-11	ave	1	39.89	183	-63.89	93
HH-4-11	day	1	39.82	221	-34.04	121
HH-4-11	joc	1	38.17	186	-1.44	94
HH-4-11	cou	1	37.08	89	-0.46	46
HH-4-11	pla	2	36.63	172	-38.22	90
HH-4-11	ave	2	35.83	240	4.76	114
HH-4-11	wei	3	34.74	285	-10.42	147
HH-4-11	tra	1	34.19	155	-61.78	81
HH-4-11	dis	1	33.85	260	-57.72	149
HH-4-11	wei	4	33.33	180	-23.39	105
HH-4-11	pla	3	32.76	174	-53.40	91
HH-4-11	rat	7	32.56	43	-2.40	29
HH-4-11	ave	3	31.71	205	-61.81	112
HH-4-11	wei	2	31.58	285	-80.25	150
HH-4-11	rat	3	31.41	191	-87.57	98
HH-4-11	pla	4	31.25	160	-30.50	86

Handicap Hurdle 12+ runners (69 Races Analysed)

race type	category	position	%	num	profit/loss	num
HH-12+	rat	1	36.23	69	-26.22	26
HH-12+	ave	1	34.34	99	-10.72	36
HH-12+	pla	2	27.27	143	-44.97	53
HH-12+	pla	1	26.80	153	-33.28	59
HH-12+	rat	2	26.40	197	-32.09	70
HH-12+	day	2	25.74	237	-35.13	81
HH-12+	pla	9	25.00	28	60.25	14
HH-12+	rat	3	24.74	194	20.00	65
HH-12+	wei	4	24.73	186	-44.81	86
HH-12+	pla	3	24.65	142	-33.25	45
HH-12+	ave	2	24.51	204	-9.78	65
HH-12+	day	1	23.17	164	-61.59	70
HH-12+	tra	1	22.60	208	-76.78	69
HH-12+	cou	1	22.22	108	5.38	34
HH-12+	dis	1	21.94	360	-21.34	108
HH-12+	day	3	21.50	200	-31.09	77
HH-12+	rat	4	21.33	150	-8.63	49
HH-12+	wei	2	21.32	319	-2.25	103

PLACE ONLY PERCENTAGE

Non Handicap Hurdle 4-11 runners (119 Races Analysed)

race type	category	position	%	num	profit/loss	num
NH-4-11	rat	1	75.63	119	-22.31	58
NH-4-11	ave	1	61.90	189	2.87	93
NH-4-11	rat	2	57.04	135	4.29	67
NH-4-11	pla	1	56.31	206	-63.69	101
NH-4-11	cou	1	52.50	40	-6.96	17
NH-4-11	tra	1	50.22	223	23.62	88
NH-4-11	pla	2	49.72	177	21.20	86
NH-4-11	ave	2	48.47	196	47.51	89
NH-4-11	dis	1	45.74	129	-51.38	61
NH-4-11	wei	3	45.59	136	-60.33	52
NH-4-11	joc	1	45.05	273	-35.41	119
NH-4-11	day	1	35.16	256	4.75	128
NH-4-11	rat	3	34.16	161	-48.31	80
NH-4-11	day	2	33.94	274	-79.37	144
NH-4-11	wei	2	30.76	543	-143.70	259
NH-4-11	day	3	30.58	206	-102.16	104
NH-4-11	pla	3	30.27	185	-40.83	81
NH-4-11	day	7	26.67	15	n/a	3

Non Handicap Hurdle 12+ runners (67 Races Analysed)

race type	category	position	%	num	profit/loss	num
NH-12+	rat	1	58.21	67	-17.67	32
NH-12+	wei	4	54.55	11	n/a	4
NH-12+	rat	2	50.65	77	-7.70	37
NH-12+	ave	1	43.90	123	-9.56	51
NH-12+	cou	1	41.18	34	-17.70	18
NH-12+	pla	2	36.84	133	-27.43	62
NH-12+	rat	3	36.14	83	-25.18	35
NH-12+	pla	1	34.23	149	-42.00	61
NH-12+	joc	1	33.70	181	-12.95	76
NH-12+	ave	2	29.44	180	-56.54	70
NH-12+	dis	1	29.41	119	-40.00	48
NH-12+	tra	1	28.11	185	-39.45	77
NH-12+	wei	3	27.83	115	-15.22	48
NH-12+	ave	3	26.97	178	-52.77	89
NH-12+	rat	4	25.81	93	11.80	46
NH-12+	pla	3	25.00	132	-68.14	67
NH-12+	day	4	24.48	143	37.41	66
NH-12+	day	3	23.90	159	-25.82	66

PLACE ONLY PERCENTAGE

Handicap Chase 4-11 runners (153 Races Analysed)

race type	category	position	%	num	profit/loss	num
HCH-4-11	pla	1	46.12	245	-49.55	105
HCH-4-11	ave	1	44.44	234	-44.88	93
HCH-4-11	day	7	40.00	10	n/a	1
HCH-4-11	joc	1	38.52	283	6.24	105
HCH-4-11	rat	1	37.91	153	-41.88	62
HCH-4-11	tra	1	36.90	252	-15.77	84
HCH-4-11	rat	3	36.78	261	-76.76	104
HCH-4-11	cou	1	36.68	199	-5.97	94
HCH-4-11	rat	2	35.80	324	-39.03	132
HCH-4-11	wei	3	35.47	375	-33.53	149
HCH-4-11	day	1	33.89	357	-41.42	159
HCH-4-11	ave	3	33.45	275	-52.00	112
HCH-4-11	day	2	32.93	334	-101.88	147
HCH-4-11	ave	2	32.50	280	-45.34	113
HCH-4-11	wei	2	32.42	364	-88.13	157
HCH-4-11	pla	2	31.91	235	-65.02	91
HCH-4-11	dis	1	31.16	414	-111.81	191
HCH-4-11	day	4	30.91	165	-42.80	65

Handicap Chase 12+ runners (51 Races Analysed)

race type	category	position	%	num	profit/loss	num
HCH-12+	pla	2	31.82	110	40.70	45
HCH-12+	ave	1	27.64	123	-22.63	40
HCH-12+	pla	1	26.09	138	-4.13	59
HCH-12+	rat	5	25.27	91	4.00	35
HCH-12+	day	4	25.23	107	-16.56	42
HCH-12+	rat	2	25.00	136	-24.94	48
HCH-12+	ave	2	24.70	166	31.76	68
HCH-12+	joc	1	24.65	142	-20.19	56
HCH-12+	day	8	23.81	21	n/a	5
HCH-12+	day	1	23.74	139	35.70	60
HCH-12+	wei	3	23.44	192	-45.25	83
HCH-12+	ave	4	23.36	137	0.13	51
HCH-12+	rat	3	22.90	131	-18.00	49
HCH-12+	rat	8	22.58	31	-7.00	13
HCH-12+	pla	3	22.22	99	1.88	43
HCH-12+	day	2	22.16	176	-43.38	63
HCH-12+	rat	1	21.57	51	-24.30	21
HCH-12+	pla	4	21.19	118	-74.00	39

PLACE ONLY PERCENTAGE

Non Handicap Chase 4-11 runners (75 Races Analysed)

race type	category	position	%	num	profit/loss	num
NCH4-11	rat	1	68.00	75	-2.88	25
NCH4-11	wei	3	52.38	21	n/a	7
NCH4-11	pla	1	51.64	122	-5.76	41
NCH4-11	dis	1	48.28	87	12.74	28
NCH4-11	ave	1	47.90	119	-26.53	42
NCH4-11	joc	1	44.87	156	-33.41	53
NCH4-11	tra	1	44.44	126	-20.79	39
NCH4-11	ave	2	37.69	130	-25.85	43
NCH4-11	pla	2	36.79	106	-32.82	34
NCH4-11	day	2	36.54	156	-40.63	54
NCH4-11	rat	2	36.28	113	-21.49	40
NCH4-11	cou	1	35.14	37	0.24	17
NCH4-11	wei	2	34.69	196	-52.88	65
NCH4-11	day	3	34.62	104	-19.85	29
NCH4-11	day	1	33.33	141	-40.36	62
NCH4-11	ave	3	32.50	120	-12.42	43

Non Handicap Chase 12+ runners (11 Races Analysed)

NOTE: - THIS IS A LOW NUMBER OF RACES ANALYSED

race type	category	position	%	num	profit/loss	num
NCH12+	rat	1	63.64	11	n/a	2
NCH12+	rat	2	53.33	15	n/a	5
NCH12+	cou	1	40.00	15	n/a	5
NCH12+	ave	1	35.48	31	n/a	6
NCH12+	tra	1	34.09	44	4.95	11
NCH12+	joc	1	32.43	37	n/a	6
NCH12+	day	1	30.77	26	n/a	5
NCH12+	day	2	30.43	23	n/a	7
NCH12+	pla	1	30.30	33	n/a	6
NCH12+	pla	2	26.92	26	n/a	6
NCH12+	ave	3	26.47	34	n/a	7
NCH12+	rat	7	25.00	16	n/a	6
NCH12+	wei	1	24.49	49	n/a	3
NCH12+	dis	1	24.24	33	-12.85	12
NCH12+	rat	5	23.08	26	n/a	4
NCH12+	day	3	22.86	35	n/a	4
NCH12+	wei	2	21.59	88	-22.20	22
NCH12+	day	6	21.43	14	n/a	2

PLACE ONLY PERCENTAGE

Handicap All Weather 4-11 runners (141 Races Analysed)

race type	category	position	%	num	profit/loss	num
HAW4-11	ave	1	46.45	211	-66.22	105
HAW4-11	rat	1	45.39	141	-40.54	71
HAW4-11	pla	1	45.15	237	-34.63	120
HAW4-11	tra	1	40.26	154	-48.64	69
HAW4-11	rat	2	39.54	306	-45.12	148
HAW4-11	ave	2	39.45	256	-25.90	126
HAW4-11	pla	3	38.69	199	4.98	102
HAW4-11	wei	3	37.12	299	-145.55	168
HAW4-11	dis	1	35.90	688	-182.14	323
HAW4-11	day	1	34.71	340	-101.16	168
HAW4-11	pla	2	34.52	197	-74.80	100
HAW4-11	cou	1	34.22	526	-124.26	243
HAW4-11	joc	1	33.46	257	-2.92	113
HAW4-11	day	2	33.06	369	-70.09	178
HAW4-11	day	4	32.35	170	-12.99	89
HAW4-11	wei	2	30.83	532	-148.87	264
HAW4-11	rat	3	30.72	319	76.61	154
HAW4-11	wei	4	30.61	49	32.14	16

Handicap All Weather 12+ runners (79 Races Analysed)

race type	category	position	%	num	profit/loss	num
HAW12+	rat	1	48.10	79	4.91	33
HAW12+	pla	1	44.52	155	21.44	60
HAW12+	wei	4	41.18	17	n/a	5
HAW12+	ave	1	36.00	125	-58.47	60
HAW12+	day	1	32.52	206	-43.16	88
HAW12+	joc	1	31.44	194	-25.88	70
HAW12+	tra	1	31.25	112	-45.31	46
HAW12+	day	6	31.03	58	3.75	31
HAW12+	cou	1	29.54	325	-19.16	146
HAW12+	dis	1	28.85	461	-16.47	220
HAW12+	ave	2	28.13	160	12.44	72
HAW12+	rat	2	28.08	203	-66.50	95
HAW12+	ave	3	27.53	178	-52.25	75
HAW12+	pla	2	25.00	136	-26.00	55
HAW12+	wei	3	24.86	177	-43.81	81
HAW12+	wei	2	24.85	491	-145.37	217
HAW12+	rat	3	23.55	242	-40.34	96
HAW12+	ave	4	23.26	172	34.60	67

PLACE ONLY PERCENTAGE

Non Handicap All Weather 4-11 runners (84 Races Analysed)

race type	category	position	%	num	profit/loss	num
NAW4-11	rat	1	70.24	84	13.73	30
NAW4-11	ave	1	57.38	122	-1.54	41
NAW4-11	pla	1	49.59	121	-15.44	41
NAW4-11	rat	2	47.92	96	-7.19	35
NAW4-11	tra	1	46.00	100	2.74	30
NAW4-11	pla	2	45.93	135	-18.47	51
NAW4-11	ave	2	44.22	147	11.10	57
NAW4-11	cou	1	40.51	79	-0.06	33
NAW4-11	joc	1	37.97	158	-17.85	47
NAW4-11	dis	1	37.93	116	-10.74	46
NAW4-11	day	2	35.00	200	-28.15	78
NAW4-11	wei	2	33.93	333	-35.29	120
NAW4-11	day	1	32.43	148	7.95	51
NAW4-11	rat	3	32.04	103	-47.71	42
NAW4-11	day	3	30.46	174	-63.06	55
NAW4-11	wei	1	30.18	338	-105.06	127
NAW4-11	pla	3	29.11	158	2.51	45
NAW4-11	day	4	28.93	121	-58.82	52

Non Handicap All Weather 12+ runners (37 Races Analysed)

race type	category	position	%	num	profit/loss	num
NAW12+	rat	1	59.46	37	n/a	8
NAW12+	pla	1	49.12	57	-0.03	11
NAW12+	ave	1	46.88	64	4.58	14
NAW12+	rat	2	38.46	52	n/a	9
NAW12+	joc	1	38.18	110	-9.70	22
NAW12+	rat	3	37.50	48	n/a	9
NAW12+	tra	1	34.78	69	-9.73	11
NAW12+	ave	2	32.93	82	-10.90	16
NAW12+	pla	3	31.15	61	-0.40	14
NAW12+	wei	3	28.57	21	n/a	7
NAW12+	rat	4	28.57	49	n/a	9
NAW12+	pla	2	28.36	67	1.80	12
NAW12+	dis	1	28.17	71	-13.23	12
NAW12+	wei	2	27.44	164	-14.65	26
NAW12+	day	1	26.80	97	-18.10	25
NAW12+	cou	1	26.53	49	n/a	4
NAW12+	rat	5	25.58	43	n/a	9
NAW12+	pla	4	25.40	63	-18.63	10

PLACE ONLY PERCENTAGE

Handicap Flat 4-11 runners (168 Races Analysed)

race type	category	position	%	num	profit/loss	num
HFL-4-11	rat	1	45.24	168	-17.14	61
HFL-4-11	tra	1	42.68	239	-43.94	105
HFL-4-11	ave	1	41.64	269	-54.63	96
HFL-4-11	pla	1	41.10	292	-51.89	101
HFL-4-11	cou	1	37.13	202	29.97	81
HFL-4-11	day	1	36.93	417	-56.06	158
HFL-4-11	rat	2	36.89	347	-4.39	131
HFL-4-11	wei	4	36.61	112	-10.28	19
HFL-4-11	joc	1	35.57	388	-40.66	138
HFL-4-11	dis	1	34.07	722	-186.27	291
HFL-4-11	wei	3	33.90	413	-57.77	144
HFL-4-11	ave	2	32.43	296	-43.30	108
HFL-4-11	pla	3	32.26	248	-47.92	90
HFL-4-11	pla	2	31.67	240	-65.78	88
HFL-4-11	ave	3	31.49	308	-55.60	121
HFL-4-11	day	6	31.43	35	-0.20	10
HFL-4-11	wei	2	31.17	571	-109.93	235
HFL-4-11	day	2	31.04	422	-74.72	161

Handicap Flat 12+ runners (56 Races Analysed)

race type	category	position	%	num	profit/loss	num
HFL-12+	pla	1	35.79	95	-11.91	38
HFL-12+	rat	1	33.93	56	-17.91	22
HFL-12+	pla	3	32.43	111	-4.81	49
HFL-12+	ave	1	31.18	93	-0.03	36
HFL-12+	joc	1	29.75	158	5.00	47
HFL-12+	tra	1	29.09	110	-35.00	40
HFL-12+	ave	2	28.97	145	-20.50	61
HFL-12+	cou	1	26.32	114	-48.00	37
HFL-12+	day	2	25.74	202	-58.31	64
HFL-12+	rat	2	25.61	164	-15.44	69
HFL-12+	wei	3	25.12	215	-25.56	83
HFL-12+	day	6	25.00	52	30.00	15
HFL-12+	dis	1	24.36	390	-69.09	154
HFL-12+	pla	2	24.27	103	-28.69	39
HFL-12+	pla	5	23.86	88	5.75	32
HFL-12+	rat	3	23.12	199	-37.25	76
HFL-12+	wei	2	23.05	308	16.94	111
HFL-12+	rat	4	22.94	170	-31.63	53

PLACE ONLY PERCENTAGE

Non Handicap Flat 4-11 runners (126 Races Analysed)

race type	category	position	%	num	profit/loss	num
NFL4-11	rat	1	58.73	126	-10.31	43
NFL4-11	rat	2	49.38	160	-22.46	54
NFL4-11	ave	1	46.74	184	-22.71	58
NFL4-11	pla	1	42.66	218	11.75	82
NFL4-11	joc	1	40.51	311	-37.74	79
NFL4-11	cou	1	39.77	88	-22.48	29
NFL4-11	pla	2	38.35	206	-23.39	67
NFL4-11	day	4	38.26	149	-28.48	58
NFL4-11	ave	2	38.14	215	9.82	71
NFL4-11	rat	3	36.65	161	34.30	55
NFL4-11	tra	1	35.98	189	-60.47	66
NFL4-11	wei	2	34.12	422	-47.07	116
NFL4-11	pla	3	34.05	185	-35.86	59
NFL4-11	dis	1	33.46	260	-43.83	95
NFL4-11	day	1	32.95	261	-64.28	91
NFL4-11	ave	3	32.92	243	-58.31	87
NFL4-11	day	2	30.81	357	-68.37	127
NFL4-11	wei	1	30.33	610	-162.09	239

Non Handicap Flat 12+ runners (29 Races Analysed)

race type	category	position	%	num	profit/loss	num
NFL12+	rat	1	68.97	29	1.43	15
NFL12+	ave	1	42.00	50	-0.45	21
NFL12+	rat	2	39.47	38	-15.36	19
NFL12+	pla	1	33.90	59	2.16	36
NFL12+	pla	3	30.36	56	-22.18	25
NFL12+	joc	1	29.70	101	-34.55	51
NFL12+	rat	6	27.78	36	22.80	15
NFL12+	tra	1	27.03	74	-26.74	45
NFL12+	rat	3	27.03	37	-22.90	19
NFL12+	day	2	27.00	100	-38.76	60
NFL12+	ave	3	25.71	70	-38.10	37
NFL12+	pla	5	25.00	44	-18.40	21
NFL12+	cou	1	25.00	20	16.20	10
NFL12+	day	3	24.69	81	-55.32	36
NFL12+	ave	2	24.36	78	-29.17	37
NFL12+	wei	2	24.35	193	-77.27	86
NFL12+	day	4	23.73	59	-30.94	34
NFL12+	dis	1	23.61	72	-24.74	41

PLACE ONLY PERCENTAGE

Best Of all Race Types/Categories (1374 Races Analysed)

race type	category	position	%	num	profit/loss	num
NH-4-11	rat	1	**75.63**	119	-22.31	58
NAW4-11	rat	1	**70.24**	84	13.73	30
NFL12+	rat	1	**68.97**	29	1.43	15
NCH4-11	rat	1	**68.00**	75	-2.88	25
NCH12+	rat	1	**63.64**	11	n/a	2
NH-4-11	ave	1	**61.90**	189	2.87	93
NAW12+	rat	1	**59.46**	37	n/a	8
NFL4-11	rat	1	**58.73**	126	-10.31	43
NH-12+	rat	1	**58.21**	67	-17.67	32
HH-4-11	rat	1	**58**	109	-28	57
NAW4-11	ave	1	**57.38**	122	-1.54	41
NH-4-11	rat	2	**57.04**	135	4.29	67
NH-4-11	pla	1	**56.31**	206	-63.69	101
NH-12+	wei	4	**54.55**	11	n/a	4
NCH12+	rat	2	**53.33**	15	n/a	5
NH-4-11	cou	1	**52.50**	40	-6.96	17
NCH4-11	wei	3	**52.38**	21	n/a	7
NCH4-11	pla	1	**51.64**	122	-5.76	41
NH-12+	rat	2	**50.65**	77	-7.70	37
NH-4-11	tra	1	**50.22**	223	23.62	88
NH-4-11	pla	2	**49.72**	177	21.20	86
NAW4-11	pla	1	**49.59**	121	-15.44	41
NFL4-11	rat	2	**49.38**	160	-22.46	54
NAW12+	pla	1	**49.12**	57	-0.03	11
NH-4-11	ave	2	**48.47**	196	47.51	89
NCH4-11	dis	1	**48.28**	87	12.74	28
HAW12+	rat	1	**48.10**	79	4.91	33
NAW4-11	rat	2	**47.92**	96	-7.19	35
NCH4-11	ave	1	**47.90**	119	-26.53	42
NAW12+	ave	1	**46.88**	64	4.58	14
NFL4-11	ave	1	**46.74**	184	-22.71	58
HAW4-11	ave	1	**46.45**	211	-66.22	105
HCH-4-11	pla	1	**46.12**	245	-49.55	105
NAW4-11	tra	1	**46.00**	100	2.74	30
NAW4-11	pla	2	**45.93**	135	-18.47	51

31

PROFIT/LOSS TABLES WIN ONLY

Please note that Non Handicap Chase 12+ runners and Non Handicap All Weather 12+ runners have been omitted from the following tables. There were less than 10 examples of these races to analyse. All profit/loss margins are shown to a £1 stake. The following profit/loss margins are for horses that won only.

WIN ONLY PROFIT/LOSS

Handicap Hurdle 4-11 runners (57 Races Analysed)

race type	category	position	profit/loss	num
HH-4-11	cou	1	17.28	46
HH-4-11	day	6	17.00	25
HH-4-11	rat	5	9.05	69
HH-4-11	joc	1	7.80	94
HH-4-11	pla	7	5.50	32
HH-4-11	rat	7	1.00	29
HH-4-11	wei	3	0.53	147
HH-4-11	day	5	0.00	65
HH-4-11	pla	1	-4.02	84
HH-4-11	ave	2	-5.72	114
HH-4-11	rat	8	-11.00	17
HH-4-11	day	1	-11.92	121
HH-4-11	wei	4	-11.97	105
HH-4-11	dis	1	-13.05	149
HH-4-11	pla	4	-13.50	86
HH-4-11	rat	4	-13.75	83
HH-4-11	rat	6	-14.25	61
HH-4-11	ave	4	-15.75	99

Handicap Hurdle 12+ runners (26 Races Analysed)

race type	category	position	profit/loss	num
HH-12+	pla	9	41.00	14
HH-12+	rat	3	37.00	65
HH-12+	ave	6	26.00	46
HH-12+	day	6	15.50	27
HH-12+	day	5	15.00	42
HH-12+	wei	2	14.50	103
HH-12+	rat	9	8.00	21
HH-12+	ave	1	3.88	36
HH-12+	pla	7	-0.50	26
HH-12+	rat	10	-2.00	13
HH-12+	pla	6	-3.00	52
HH-12+	cou	1	-6.00	34
HH-12+	pla	4	-6.25	57
HH-12+	ave	2	-7.70	65
HH-12+	dis	1	-8.50	108
HH-12+	ave	4	-10.50	65
HH-12+	rat	4	-11.00	49
HH-12+	rat	1	-12.58	26

33

WIN ONLY PROFIT/LOSS

Non Handicap Hurdle 4-11 runners (58 Races Analysed)

race type	category	position	profit/loss	num
NH-4-11	ave	2	**38.38**	89
NH-4-11	pla	2	**20.54**	86
NH-4-11	rat	2	**6.51**	67
NH-4-11	ave	1	**3.94**	93
NH-4-11	tra	1	**2.40**	88
NH-4-11	rat	4	**-3.75**	90
NH-4-11	cou	1	**-4.20**	17
NH-4-11	day	1	**-8.67**	128
NH-4-11	ave	7	**-16.50**	21
NH-4-11	pla	7	**-17.00**	17
NH-4-11	rat	8	**-17.00**	17
NH-4-11	rat	1	**-21.68**	58
NH-4-11	day	6	**-22.00**	22
NH-4-11	pla	3	**-23.63**	81
NH-4-11	rat	3	**-29.63**	80
NH-4-11	joc	1	**-30.52**	119
NH-4-11	pla	6	**-31.75**	57
NH-4-11	day	5	**-32.50**	54

Non Handicap Hurdle 12+ runners (32 Races Analysed)

race type	category	position	profit/loss	num
NH-12+	day	4	**46.14**	66
NH-12+	pla	5	**14.50**	55
NH-12+	joc	1	**7.19**	76
NH-12+	ave	7	**6.00**	28
NH-12+	pla	4	**3.00**	63
NH-12+	rat	4	**1.50**	46
NH-12+	ave	4	**0.00**	71
NH-12+	wei	3	**-1.37**	48
NH-12+	rat	2	**-4.25**	37
NH-12+	ave	1	**-5.28**	51
NH-12+	rat	6	**-9.12**	46
NH-12+	rat	1	**-11.75**	32
NH-12+	rat	10	**-13.00**	13
NH-12+	day	8	**-14.00**	14
NH-12+	cou	1	**-14.77**	18
NH-12+	day	7	**-17.00**	28
NH-12+	rat	8	**-19.00**	38
NH-12+	rat	3	**-20.50**	35

WIN ONLY PROFIT/LOSS

Handicap Chase 4-11 runners (62 Races Analysed)

race type	category	position	profit/loss	num
HCH-4-11	joc	1	12.58	105
HCH-4-11	pla	5	10.50	73
HCH-4-11	tra	1	2.38	84
HCH-4-11	cou	1	1.13	94
HCH-4-11	rat	6	0.50	46
HCH-4-11	day	5	-1.00	43
HCH-4-11	wei	3	-2.38	149
HCH-4-11	ave	6	-3.17	28
HCH-4-11	pla	7	-3.67	18
HCH-4-11	wei	4	-6.04	71
HCH-4-11	ave	2	-8.38	113
HCH-4-11	rat	7	-9.00	21
HCH-4-11	pla	3	-14.25	101
HCH-4-11	rat	2	-19.13	132
HCH-4-11	rat	1	-19.95	62
HCH-4-11	rat	5	-20.79	72
HCH-4-11	day	1	-21.88	159
HCH-4-11	pla	6	-22.00	35

Handicap Chase 12+ runners (21 Races Analysed)

race type	category	position	profit/loss	num
HCH-12+	ave	2	31.50	68
HCH-12+	day	1	20.75	60
HCH-12+	pla	2	20.50	45
HCH-12+	rat	4	18.00	45
HCH-12+	rat	5	9.00	35
HCH-12+	wei	1	7.75	74
HCH-12+	pla	3	4.00	43
HCH-12+	pla	1	3.25	59
HCH-12+	rat	9	-2.50	12
HCH-12+	day	5	-3.00	37
HCH-12+	day	7	-6.00	13
HCH-12+	day	4	-7.00	42
HCH-12+	ave	4	-9.00	51
HCH-12+	rat	3	-10.00	49
HCH-12+	ave	1	-11.75	40
HCH-12+	rat	1	-12.25	21
HCH-12+	ave	6	-12.50	22
HCH-12+	wei	2	-13.00	66

WIN ONLY PROFIT/LOSS

Non Handicap Chase 4-11 runners (25 Races Analysed)

race type	category	position	profit/loss	num
NCH-4-11	rat	1	2.32	25
NCH-4-11	day	4	0.25	25
NCH-4-11	rat	6	-1.00	11
NCH-4-11	pla	1	-1.57	41
NCH-4-11	dis	1	-3.01	28
NCH-4-11	rat	3	-4.15	26
NCH-4-11	cou	1	-7.43	17
NCH-4-11	pla	3	-9.26	40
NCH-4-11	ave	3	-11.50	43
NCH-4-11	tra	1	-11.50	39
NCH-4-11	pla	6	-13.00	13
NCH-4-11	rat	2	-14.00	40
NCH-4-11	ave	5	-14.33	16
NCH-4-11	ave	4	-15.50	30
NCH-4-11	ave	1	-15.98	42
NCH-4-11	pla	2	-17.00	34
NCH-4-11	day	3	-18.75	29
NCH-4-11	day	2	-19.58	54

WIN ONLY PROFIT/LOSS

Handicap All Weather 4-11 runners (71 Races Analysed)

race type	category	position	profit/loss	num
HAW-4-11	rat	3	95.50	154
HAW-4-11	wei	4	29.50	16
HAW-4-11	ave	5	24.74	87
HAW-4-11	wei	1	20.10	173
HAW-4-11	day	3	14.35	118
HAW-4-11	joc	1	10.74	113
HAW-4-11	pla	3	3.38	102
HAW-4-11	ave	2	-0.40	126
HAW-4-11	pla	6	-2.17	70
HAW-4-11	ave	6	-3.00	44
HAW-4-11	day	4	-6.42	89
HAW-4-11	pla	5	-14.00	81
HAW-4-11	day	6	-15.00	15
HAW-4-11	pla	1	-16.10	120
HAW-4-11	ave	7	-23.00	23
HAW-4-11	rat	7	-25.00	25
HAW-4-11	rat	1	-25.78	71
HAW-4-11	pla	4	-32.50	100

Handicap All Weather Hurdle 12+ runners (33 Races Analysed)

race type	category	position	profit/loss	num
HAW-12+	pla	6	122.00	61
HAW-12+	wei	1	105.00	121
HAW-12+	ave	5	93.00	73
HAW-12+	rat	6	89.00	33
HAW-12+	day	5	82.00	33
HAW-12+	ave	4	34.38	67
HAW-12+	day	2	32.88	127
HAW-12+	rat	1	15.13	33
HAW-12+	ave	2	14.75	72
HAW-12+	pla	1	13.26	60
HAW-12+	cou	1	8.13	146
HAW-12+	rat	4	0.00	75
HAW-12+	day	6	-1.50	31
HAW-12+	rat	7	-2.00	23
HAW-12+	dis	1	-4.13	220
HAW-12+	pla	5	-12.00	58
HAW-12+	rat	8	-14.00	14
HAW-12+	wei	3	-15.50	81

WIN ONLY PROFIT/LOSS

Non Handicap All Weather 4-11 runners (30 Races Analysed)

race type	category	position	profit/loss	num
NAW-4-11	rat	4	42.00	42
NAW-4-11	pla	4	17.50	43
NAW-4-11	day	1	9.85	51
NAW-4-11	rat	1	9.12	30
NAW-4-11	day	5	9.00	19
NAW-4-11	ave	3	6.10	56
NAW-4-11	ave	2	5.13	57
NAW-4-11	tra	1	4.25	30
NAW-4-11	cou	1	1.25	33
NAW-4-11	dis	1	0.75	46
NAW-4-11	pla	3	-5.50	45
NAW-4-11	ave	1	-6.23	41
NAW-4-11	rat	2	-9.75	35
NAW-4-11	wei	2	-9.92	120
NAW-4-11	wei	3	-10.00	16
NAW-4-11	ave	6	-12.00	20
NAW-4-11	pla	2	-12.33	51
NAW-4-11	joc	1	-12.88	47

WIN ONLY PROFIT/LOSS

Handicap Flat 4-11 runners (61 Races Analysed)

race type	category	position	profit/loss	num
HFL-4-11	cou	1	34.05	81
HFL-4-11	pla	5	29.00	77
HFL-4-11	day	5	10.50	41
HFL-4-11	rat	2	8.10	131
HFL-4-11	day	6	-1.00	10
HFL-4-11	rat	1	-5.17	61
HFL-4-11	pla	8	-5.50	12
HFL-4-11	wei	4	-9.50	19
HFL-4-11	ave	7	-10.50	18
HFL-4-11	pla	3	-11.20	90
HFL-4-11	rat	6	-13.50	30
HFL-4-11	ave	2	-14.62	108
HFL-4-11	rat	7	-16.00	16
HFL-4-11	ave	4	-20.84	94
HFL-4-11	pla	6	-24.00	56
HFL-4-11	joc	1	-24.06	138
HFL-4-11	ave	3	-24.17	121
HFL-4-11	ave	5	-24.50	82

Handicap Flat 12+ runners (22 Races Analysed)

race type	category	position	profit/loss	num
HFL-12+	rat	5	51.75	34
HFL-12+	day	1	37.00	66
HFL-12+	pla	7	32.50	30
HFL-12+	ave	3	32.00	50
HFL-12+	day	6	26.00	15
HFL-12+	wei	2	22.50	111
HFL-12+	pla	5	22.00	32
HFL-12+	wei	4	13.00	12
HFL-12+	day	5	9.88	39
HFL-12+	ave	5	6.00	41
HFL-12+	pla	4	5.50	37
HFL-12+	joc	1	4.00	47
HFL-12+	ave	7	0.00	21
HFL-12+	rat	2	0.00	69
HFL-12+	ave	1	-2.88	36
HFL-12+	pla	3	-4.75	49
HFL-12+	wei	3	-8.75	83
HFL-12+	pla	8	-10.00	10

WIN ONLY PROFIT/LOSS

Non Handicap Flat 4-11 runners (43 Races Analysed)

race type	category	position	profit/loss	num
NFL-4-11	rat	3	26.80	55
NFL-4-11	pla	1	15.78	82
NFL-4-11	ave	5	9.25	52
NFL-4-11	ave	2	9.10	71
NFL-4-11	wei	3	-1.00	10
NFL-4-11	rat	1	-6.51	43
NFL-4-11	day	5	-9.70	14
NFL-4-11	cou	1	-10.90	29
NFL-4-11	ave	1	-11.81	58
NFL-4-11	rat	8	-13.00	13
NFL-4-11	rat	2	-14.25	54
NFL-4-11	day	4	-14.75	58
NFL-4-11	pla	6	-15.00	27
NFL-4-11	day	3	-15.13	70
NFL-4-11	pla	3	-16.75	59
NFL-4-11	wei	2	-20.72	116
NFL-4-11	ave	6	-22.00	22
NFL-4-11	dis	1	-22.85	95

Non Handicap Flat 12+ runners (15 Races Analysed)

race type	category	position	profit/loss	num
NFL-12+	rat	6	21.00	15
NFL-12+	cou	1	16.00	10
NFL-12+	pla	1	7.55	36
NFL-12+	ave	1	2.50	21
NFL-12+	rat	1	2.23	15
NFL-12+	wei	3	0.00	21
NFL-12+	dis	1	-4.12	41
NFL-12+	rat	5	-7.00	17
NFL-12+	tra	1	-7.62	45
NFL-12+	ave	7	-8.70	13
NFL-12+	pla	3	-9.37	25
NFL-12+	day	1	-10.62	41
NFL-12+	pla	5	-11.00	21
NFL-12+	day	4	-11.70	34
NFL-12+	ave	2	-11.77	37
NFL-12+	rat	2	-14.30	19
NFL-12+	pla	7	-15.00	15
NFL-12+	rat	3	-16.25	19

WIN ONLY PROFIT/LOSS

Best Of all Race Types/Categories (566 Races Analysed)

race type	category	position	profit/loss	num
HAW-12+	pla	6	122.00	61
HAW-12+	wei	1	105.00	121
HAW-4-11	rat	3	95.50	154
HAW-12+	ave	5	93.00	73
HAW-12+	rat	6	89.00	33
HAW-12+	day	5	82.00	33
HFL-12+	rat	5	51.75	34
NH-12+	day	4	46.14	66
NAW-4-11	rat	4	42.00	42
HH-12+	pla	9	41.00	14
NH-4-11	ave	2	38.38	89
HH-12+	rat	3	37.00	65
HFL-12+	day	1	37.00	66
HAW-12+	ave	4	34.38	67
HFL-4-11	cou	1	34.05	81
HAW-12+	day	2	32.88	127
HFL-12+	pla	7	32.50	30
HFL-12+	ave	3	32.00	50
HCH-12+	ave	2	31.50	68
HAW-4-11	wei	4	29.50	16
HFL-4-11	pla	5	29.00	77
NFL-4-11	rat	3	26.80	55
HH-12+	ave	6	26.00	46
HFL-12+	day	6	26.00	15
HAW-4-11	ave	5	24.74	87
HFL-12+	wei	2	22.50	111
HFL-12+	pla	5	22.00	32
NFL-12+	rat	6	21.00	15
HCH-12+	day	1	20.75	60
NH-4-11	pla	2	20.54	86
HCH-12+	pla	2	20.50	45
HAW-4-11	wei	1	20.10	173
HCH-12+	rat	4	18.00	45
NAW-4-11	pla	4	17.50	43
HH-4-11	cou	1	17	46

WIN AND PLACE (E/W) PROFIT/LOSS

Please note that Non Handicap Chase 12+ runners and Non Handicap All Weather 12+ runners have been omitted from the following tables. There were less than 10 examples of these races to analyse. The following tables include the profit/loss margins for horses that either won or were placed i.e. E/W - each way.

WIN AND PLACE (E/W) PROFIT/LOSS

Handicap Hurdle 4-11 runners (57 Races Analysed)

race type	category	position	profit/loss	num
HH-4-11	day	6	8.50	25
HH-4-11	ave	2	4.76	114
HH-4-11	day	5	0.73	65
HH-4-11	cou	1	-0.46	46
HH-4-11	joc	1	-1.44	94
HH-4-11	rat	5	-2.13	69
HH-4-11	rat	7	-2.40	29
HH-4-11	pla	7	-6.50	32
HH-4-11	wei	3	-10.42	147
HH-4-11	rat	8	-18.00	17
HH-4-11	pla	1	-21.77	84
HH-4-11	wei	4	-23.39	105
HH-4-11	rat	4	-23.40	83
HH-4-11	rat	1	-28.22	57
HH-4-11	pla	4	-30.50	86
HH-4-11	day	1	-34.04	121
HH-4-11	rat	6	-34.60	61
HH-4-11	pla	2	-38.22	90

Handicap Hurdle 12+ runners (26 Races Analysed)

race type	category	position	profit/loss	num
HH-12+	pla	9	60.25	14
HH-12+	ave	6	27.63	46
HH-12+	rat	3	20.00	65
HH-12+	day	6	16.38	27
HH-12+	cou	1	5.38	34
HH-12+	rat	9	5.25	21
HH-12+	day	5	3.50	42
HH-12+	wei	2	-2.25	103
HH-12+	rat	4	-8.63	49
HH-12+	rat	10	-8.75	13
HH-12+	pla	7	-9.25	26
HH-12+	ave	2	-9.78	65
HH-12+	ave	1	-10.72	36
HH-12+	pla	6	-20.63	52
HH-12+	dis	1	-21.34	108
HH-12+	rat	1	-26.22	26
HH-12+	day	7	-30.00	15
HH-12+	day	3	-31.09	77

WIN AND PLACE (E/W) PROFIT/LOSS

Non Handicap Hurdle 4-11 runners (58 Races Analysed)

race type	category	position	profit/loss	num
NH-4-11	ave	2	47.51	89
NH-4-11	tra	1	23.62	88
NH-4-11	pla	2	21.20	86
NH-4-11	day	1	4.75	128
NH-4-11	rat	2	4.29	67
NH-4-11	ave	1	2.87	93
NH-4-11	cou	1	-6.96	17
NH-4-11	rat	4	-10.71	90
NH-4-11	ave	5	-18.03	72
NH-4-11	rat	1	-22.31	58
NH-4-11	day	6	-31.60	22
NH-4-11	ave	7	-32.00	21
NH-4-11	pla	7	-34.00	17
NH-4-11	rat	8	-34.00	17
NH-4-11	joc	1	-35.41	119
NH-4-11	day	5	-37.04	54
NH-4-11	pla	3	-40.83	81
NH-4-11	rat	5	-45.00	97

Non Handicap Hurdle 12+ runners (32 Races Analysed)

race type	category	position	profit/loss	num
NH-12+	day	4	37.41	66
NH-12+	pla	5	21.00	55
NH-12+	rat	4	11.80	46
NH-12+	rat	2	-7.70	37
NH-12+	ave	1	-9.56	51
NH-12+	ave	7	-11.00	28
NH-12+	joc	1	-12.95	76
NH-12+	wei	3	-15.22	48
NH-12+	pla	4	-17.28	63
NH-12+	rat	1	-17.67	32
NH-12+	cou	1	-17.70	18
NH-12+	rat	10	-22.60	13
NH-12+	day	8	-24.20	14
NH-12+	rat	3	-25.18	35
NH-12+	day	3	-25.82	66
NH-12+	ave	4	-26.60	71
NH-12+	pla	2	-27.43	62
NH-12+	day	6	-30.70	45

WIN AND PLACE (E/W) PROFIT/LOSS

Handicap Chase 4-11 runners (62 Races Analysed)

race type	category	position	profit/loss	num
HCH-4-11	joc	1	6.24	105
HCH-4-11	pla	5	-2.65	73
HCH-4-11	cou	1	-5.97	94
HCH-4-11	rat	6	-11.88	46
HCH-4-11	pla	7	-12.60	18
HCH-4-11	ave	6	-13.35	28
HCH-4-11	tra	1	-15.77	84
HCH-4-11	rat	7	-16.60	21
HCH-4-11	day	5	-18.93	43
HCH-4-11	wei	4	-22.60	71
HCH-4-11	pla	3	-22.76	101
HCH-4-11	pla	6	-29.80	35
HCH-4-11	rat	5	-31.63	72
HCH-4-11	wei	3	-33.53	149
HCH-4-11	rat	2	-39.03	132
HCH-4-11	day	1	-41.42	159
HCH-4-11	rat	1	-41.88	62
HCH-4-11	day	4	-42.80	65

Handicap Chase 12+ runners (21 Races Analysed)

race type	category	position	profit/loss	num
HCH-12+	pla	2	40.70	45
HCH-12+	day	1	35.70	60
HCH-12+	ave	2	31.76	68
HCH-12+	rat	4	18.50	45
HCH-12+	rat	5	4.00	35
HCH-12+	pla	3	1.88	43
HCH-12+	ave	4	0.13	51
HCH-12+	pla	1	-4.13	59
HCH-12+	wei	1	-4.31	74
HCH-12+	rat	9	-6.38	12
HCH-12+	rat	8	-7.00	13
HCH-12+	day	7	-9.50	13
HCH-12+	day	4	-16.56	42
HCH-12+	rat	3	-18.00	49
HCH-12+	joc	1	-20.19	56
HCH-12+	day	6	-22.00	14
HCH-12+	ave	1	-22.63	40
HCH-12+	rat	1	-24.30	21

WIN AND PLACE (E/W) PROFIT/LOSS

Non Handicap Chase 4-11 runners (25 Races Analysed)

race type	category	position	profit/loss	num
NCH-4-11	dis	1	12.74	28
NCH-4-11	cou	1	0.24	17
NCH-4-11	rat	1	-2.88	25
NCH-4-11	rat	3	-3.66	26
NCH-4-11	pla	1	-5.76	41
NCH-4-11	day	4	-7.15	25
NCH-4-11	rat	6	-9.20	11
NCH-4-11	ave	3	-12.42	43
NCH-4-11	pla	4	-15.61	25
NCH-4-11	pla	6	-19.30	13
NCH-4-11	pla	3	-19.49	40
NCH-4-11	day	3	-19.85	29
NCH-4-11	ave	5	-20.40	16
NCH-4-11	tra	1	-20.79	39
NCH-4-11	rat	2	-21.49	40
NCH-4-11	ave	2	-25.85	43
NCH-4-11	ave	1	-26.53	42
NCH-4-11	pla	5	-27.23	24

WIN AND PLACE (E/W) PROFIT/LOSS

Handicap All Weather 4-11 runners (71 Races Analysed)

race type	category	position	profit/loss	num
HAW-4-11	rat	3	76.61	154
HAW-4-11	wei	4	32.14	16
HAW-4-11	ave	5	12.94	87
HAW-4-11	pla	3	4.98	102
HAW-4-11	joc	1	-2.92	113
HAW-4-11	wei	1	-5.02	173
HAW-4-11	day	3	-8.71	118
HAW-4-11	day	4	-12.99	89
HAW-4-11	day	6	-25.40	15
HAW-4-11	pla	6	-25.75	70
HAW-4-11	ave	2	-25.90	126
HAW-4-11	ave	6	-27.05	44
HAW-4-11	ave	7	-28.60	23
HAW-4-11	pla	1	-34.63	120
HAW-4-11	rat	1	-40.54	71
HAW-4-11	rat	2	-45.12	148
HAW-4-11	rat	7	-45.35	25
HAW-4-11	rat	6	-47.75	39

Handicap All Weather Hurdle 12+ runners (33 Races Analysed)

race type	category	position	profit/loss	num
HAW-12+	pla	6	144.13	61
HAW-12+	wei	1	119.25	121
HAW-12+	rat	6	112.13	33
HAW-12+	ave	5	106.38	73
HAW-12+	day	5	93.50	33
HAW-12+	ave	4	34.60	67
HAW-12+	pla	1	21.44	60
HAW-12+	ave	2	12.44	72
HAW-12+	rat	1	4.91	33
HAW-12+	day	6	3.75	31
HAW-12+	pla	5	-1.19	58
HAW-12+	rat	4	-3.88	75
HAW-12+	day	2	-4.15	127
HAW-12+	rat	7	-8.88	23
HAW-12+	rat	8	-16.25	14
HAW-12+	dis	1	-16.47	220
HAW-12+	cou	1	-19.16	146
HAW-12+	joc	1	-25.88	70

WIN AND PLACE (E/W) PROFIT/LOSS

Non Handicap All Weather 4-11 runners (30 Races Analysed)

race type	category	position	profit/loss	num
NAW-4-11	rat	4	48.33	42
NAW-4-11	rat	1	13.73	30
NAW-4-11	ave	2	11.10	57
NAW-4-11	day	1	7.95	51
NAW-4-11	pla	4	4.01	43
NAW-4-11	tra	1	2.74	30
NAW-4-11	pla	3	2.51	45
NAW-4-11	day	5	1.93	19
NAW-4-11	cou	1	-0.06	33
NAW-4-11	ave	1	-1.54	41
NAW-4-11	rat	2	-7.19	35
NAW-4-11	dis	1	-10.74	46
NAW-4-11	ave	3	-12.68	56
NAW-4-11	wei	3	-13.00	16
NAW-4-11	pla	1	-15.44	41
NAW-4-11	joc	1	-17.85	47
NAW-4-11	pla	2	-18.47	51
NAW-4-11	rat	8	-19.80	15

WIN AND PLACE (E/W) PROFIT/LOSS

Handicap Flat 4-11 runners (61 Races Analysed)

race type	category	position	profit/loss	num
HFL-4-11	cou	1	29.97	81
HFL-4-11	pla	5	29.85	77
HFL-4-11	day	6	-0.20	10
HFL-4-11	rat	2	-4.39	131
HFL-4-11	day	5	-4.54	41
HFL-4-11	ave	7	-8.80	18
HFL-4-11	wei	4	-10.28	19
HFL-4-11	pla	8	-11.53	12
HFL-4-11	rat	1	-17.14	61
HFL-4-11	rat	7	-24.10	16
HFL-4-11	rat	6	-33.70	30
HFL-4-11	pla	7	-35.40	39
HFL-4-11	pla	6	-38.10	56
HFL-4-11	joc	1	-40.66	138
HFL-4-11	ave	5	-41.80	82
HFL-4-11	ave	2	-43.30	108
HFL-4-11	tra	1	-43.94	105
HFL-4-11	pla	3	-47.92	90

Handicap Flat 12+ runners (22 Races Analysed)

race type	category	position	profit/loss	num
HFL-12+	rat	5	53.94	34
HFL-12+	pla	7	34.63	30
HFL-12+	day	6	30.00	15
HFL-12+	ave	3	27.63	50
HFL-12+	day	1	20.81	66
HFL-12+	wei	2	16.94	111
HFL-12+	wei	4	8.75	12
HFL-12+	day	5	7.34	39
HFL-12+	pla	5	5.75	32
HFL-12+	joc	1	5.00	47
HFL-12+	ave	1	-0.03	36
HFL-12+	ave	7	-3.25	21
HFL-12+	pla	3	-4.81	49
HFL-12+	rat	6	-9.75	18
HFL-12+	pla	1	-11.91	38
HFL-12+	pla	4	-13.63	37
HFL-12+	ave	5	-14.13	41
HFL-12+	rat	2	-15.44	69

WIN AND PLACE (E/W) PROFIT/LOSS

Non Handicap Flat 4-11 runners (43 Races Analysed)

race type	category	position	profit/loss	num
NFL-4-11	rat	3	34.30	55
NFL-4-11	pla	1	11.75	82
NFL-4-11	ave	2	9.82	71
NFL-4-11	wei	3	-4.00	10
NFL-4-11	rat	1	-10.31	43
NFL-4-11	ave	5	-14.50	52
NFL-4-11	day	5	-16.04	14
NFL-4-11	rat	8	-20.60	13
NFL-4-11	rat	2	-22.46	54
NFL-4-11	cou	1	-22.48	29
NFL-4-11	ave	1	-22.71	58
NFL-4-11	pla	2	-23.39	67
NFL-4-11	pla	6	-25.20	27
NFL-4-11	day	4	-28.48	58
NFL-4-11	pla	3	-35.86	59
NFL-4-11	ave	6	-36.80	22
NFL-4-11	joc	1	-37.74	79
NFL-4-11	day	3	-40.20	70

Non Handicap Flat 12+ runners (15 Races Analysed)

race type	category	position	profit/loss	num
NFL-12+	rat	6	22.80	15
NFL-12+	cou	1	16.20	10
NFL-12+	pla	1	2.16	36
NFL-12+	rat	1	1.43	15
NFL-12+	ave	1	-0.45	21
NFL-12+	rat	5	-7.20	17
NFL-12+	wei	3	-8.25	21
NFL-12+	rat	2	-15.36	19
NFL-12+	ave	5	-15.80	27
NFL-12+	pla	5	-18.40	21
NFL-12+	ave	7	-20.04	13
NFL-12+	pla	3	-22.18	25
NFL-12+	rat	3	-22.90	19
NFL-12+	dis	1	-24.74	41
NFL-12+	day	6	-25.70	18
NFL-12+	tra	1	-26.74	45
NFL-12+	rat	4	-28.69	28
NFL-12+	ave	2	-29.17	37

WIN AND PLACE (E/W) PROFIT/LOSS

Best Of all Race Types/Categories (566 Races Analysed)

race type	category	position	profit/loss	num
HAW-12+	pla	6	144.13	61
HAW-12+	wei	1	119.25	121
HAW-12+	rat	6	112.13	33
HAW-12+	ave	5	106.38	73
HAW-12+	day	5	93.50	33
HAW-4-11	rat	3	76.61	154
HH-12+	pla	9	60.25	14
HFL-12+	rat	5	53.94	34
NAW-4-11	rat	4	48.33	42
NH-4-11	ave	2	47.51	89
HCH-12+	pla	2	40.70	45
NH-12+	day	4	37.41	66
HCH-12+	day	1	35.70	60
HFL-12+	pla	7	34.63	30
HAW-12+	ave	4	34.60	67
NFL-4-11	rat	3	34.30	55
HAW-4-11	wei	4	32.14	16
HCH-12+	ave	2	31.76	68
HFL-12+	day	6	30.00	15
HFL-4-11	cou	1	29.97	81
HFL-4-11	pla	5	29.85	77
HFL-12+	ave	3	27.63	50
HH-12+	ave	6	27.63	46
NH-4-11	tra	1	23.62	88
NFL-12+	rat	6	22.80	15
HAW-12+	pla	1	21.44	60
NH-4-11	pla	2	21.20	86
NH-12+	pla	5	21.00	55
HFL-12+	day	1	20.81	66
HH-12+	rat	3	20.00	65
HCH-12+	rat	4	18.50	45
HFL-12+	wei	2	16.94	111
HH-12+	day	6	16.38	27
NFL-12+	cou	1	16.20	10
NAW-4-11	rat	1	13.73	30

PLACE ONLY WITHOUT WIN - PROFIT/LOSS

This is a table showing the best categories in relation to place only betting. Not many people gamble using place only betting and this is not a true estimation as the odds on such betting is usually calculated by the tote. This table has only been derived by calculating normal bookmaker's odds i.e. 1/4 of bookmaker's odds for races of less than 8 runners – handicaps of more than 12 runners and a 1/5 of odds for all other races.

race type	category	position	%	num
HAW-12+	rat	6	23.13	33
HAW-12+	pla	6	22.13	61
NH-4-11	tra	1	21.21	88
HCH-12+	pla	2	20.20	45
HH-12+	pla	9	19.25	14
NH-4-11	ave	5	15.97	72
NCH-4-11	dis	1	15.75	28
HCH-12+	day	1	14.95	60
HAW-12+	wei	1	14.25	121
NH-4-11	day	1	13.42	128
HAW-12+	ave	5	13.38	73
HAW-12+	day	5	11.50	33
HH-12+	cou	1	11.38	34
HAW-12+	pla	5	10.81	58
HH-4-11	ave	2	10	114
NH-12+	rat	4	10.30	46
HH-12+	rat	2	9.91	70
NAW-12+	pla	3	9.85	14
NH-4-11	ave	2	9.13	89
HCH-12+	ave	4	9.13	51
NFL-4-11	joc	1	8.63	79
NFL-4-11	pla	2	8.35	67
HAW-12+	pla	1	8.19	60
NAW-4-11	pla	3	8.01	45
NCH-4-11	cou	1	7.67	17
NFL-4-11	rat	3	7.50	55
NAW-12+	day	4	6.60	14
NH-12+	pla	5	6.50	55
NAW-4-11	rat	4	6.33	42
HCH-12+	rat	8	6.00	13
NAW-4-11	ave	2	5.98	57
HAW-12+	day	6	5.25	31
NH-12+	pla	2	4.80	62
HH-12+	pla	3	4.75	45
HFL-12+	pla	1	4.72	38

WIN PROFIT/LOSS - COURSE, DISTANCE

race type	category	pos	win prof/loss	num	e/w prof/loss	num
HFL-4-11	cou	1	**34.05**	81	29.97	81
HH-4-11	cou	1	**17.28**	46	-0.46	46
NFL-12+	cou	1	**16.00**	10	16.20	10
HAW-12+	cou	1	**8.13**	146	-19.16	146
NAW-4-11	cou	1	**1.25**	33	-0.06	33
HCH-4-11	cou	1	**1.13**	94	-5.97	94
NH-4-11	cou	1	**-4.20**	17	-6.96	17
HH-12+	cou	1	**-6.00**	34	5.38	34
NCH-4-11	cou	1	**-7.43**	17	0.24	17
NFL-4-11	cou	1	**-10.90**	29	-22.48	29
NH-12+	cou	1	**-14.77**	18	-17.70	18
HCH-12+	cou	1	**-28.25**	51	-31.94	51
HFL-12+	cou	1	**-33.00**	37	-48.00	37
HAW-4-11	cou	1	**-91.50**	243	-124.26	243
NCH-12+	cou	1	**n/a**	5	n/a	5
NAW-12+	cou	1	**n/a**	4	n/a	4

race type	category	pos	win prof/loss	num	e/w prof/loss	num
NAW-4-11	dis	1	**0.75**	46	-10.74	46
NCH-4-11	dis	1	**-3.01**	28	12.74	28
NFL-12+	dis	1	**-4.12**	41	-24.74	41
HAW-12+	dis	1	**-4.13**	220	-16.47	220
NAW-12+	dis	1	**-5.50**	12	-13.23	12
HH-12+	dis	1	**-8.50**	108	-21.34	108
NCH-12+	dis	1	**-10.17**	12	-12.85	12
HH-4-11	dis	1	**-13.05**	149	-57.72	149
NFL-4-11	dis	1	**-22.85**	95	-43.83	95
HCH-12+	dis	1	**-25.25**	98	-53.43	98
HFL-12+	dis	1	**-26.38**	154	-69.09	154
NH-12+	dis	1	**-28.58**	48	-40.00	48
NH-4-11	dis	1	**-34.07**	61	-51.38	61
HCH-4-11	dis	1	**-67.33**	191	-111.81	191
HFL-4-11	dis	1	**-96.24**	291	-186.27	291
HAW-4-11	dis	1	**-112.13**	323	-182.14	323

WIN PROFIT/LOSS - TRAINER, JOCKEY

race type	category	pos	win prof/loss	num	e/w prof/loss	num
NAW-4-11	tra	1	**4.25**	30	2.74	30
NCH-12+	tra	1	**4.00**	11	4.95	11
NH-4-11	tra	1	**2.40**	88	23.62	88
HCH-4-11	tra	1	**2.38**	84	-15.77	84
NAW-12+	tra	1	**-6.00**	11	-9.73	11
NFL-12+	tra	1	**-7.62**	45	-26.74	45
NCH-4-11	tra	1	**-11.50**	39	-20.79	39
NH-12+	tra	1	**-23.81**	77	-39.45	77
HFL-12+	tra	1	**-26.00**	40	-35.00	40
HCH-12+	tra	1	**-30.00**	54	-42.56	54
HAW-4-11	tra	1	**-32.84**	69	-48.64	69
HH-4-11	tra	1	**-33.75**	81	-61.78	81
HAW-12+	tra	1	**-34.25**	46	-45.31	46
NFL-4-11	tra	1	**-41.42**	66	-60.47	66
HFL-4-11	tra	1	**-44.97**	105	-43.94	105
HH-12+	tra	1	**-55.25**	69	-76.78	69

race type	category	pos	win prof/loss	num	e/w prof/loss	num
HCH-4-11	joc	1	**12.58**	105	6.24	105
HAW-4-11	joc	1	**10.74**	113	-2.92	113
HH-4-11	joc	1	**7.80**	94	-1.44	94
NH-12+	joc	1	**7.19**	76	-12.95	76
HFL-12+	joc	1	**4.00**	47	5.00	47
NAW-12+	joc	1	**-7.00**	22	-9.70	22
NAW-4-11	joc	1	**-12.88**	47	-17.85	47
HAW-12+	joc	1	**-17.00**	70	-25.88	70
NFL-12+	joc	1	**-19.80**	51	-34.55	51
HCH-12+	joc	1	**-20.50**	56	-20.19	56
NCH-4-11	joc	1	**-23.82**	53	-33.41	53
HFL-4-11	joc	1	**-24.06**	138	-40.66	138
NH-4-11	joc	1	**-30.52**	119	-35.41	119
NFL-4-11	joc	1	**-46.37**	79	-37.74	79
HH-12+	joc	1	**-64.50**	73	-114.38	73
NCH-12+	joc	1	**n/a**	6	n/a	6

WIN PROFIT/LOSS - COURSE AND DISTANCE

race type	category	pos	win prof/loss	num	e/w prof/loss	num
HFL-4-11	c&d	1	**16.30**	63	-2.94	63
NF-12+	c&d	1	**16.00**	10	16.20	10
HAW-12+	c&d	1	**15.13**	121	-3.03	121
HH-4-11	c&d	1	**13.78**	32	3.54	32
NAW-4-11	c&d	1	**6.25**	28	5.64	28
HH-12+	c&d	1	**6.00**	22	20.38	22
NF-4-11	c&d	1	**-2.90**	21	-9.83	21
HCH-4-11	c&d	1	**-5.13**	68	-6.27	68
NH-4-11	c&d	1	**-9.20**	12	-9.76	12
NH-12+	c&d	1	**-9.77**	13	-8.92	13
HCH-12+	c&d	1	**-16.25**	33	-15.19	33
HFL-12+	c&d	1	**-22.00**	26	-43.25	26
HAW-4-11	c&d	1	**-69.00**	193	-100.59	193
NCH-4-11	c&d	1	**n/a**	8	n/a	8
NCH-12+	c&d	1	**n/a**	4	n/a	4
NAW-12+	c&d	1	**n/a**	4	n/a	4

GOING - BY WIN PERCENTAGE FOR ALL RACES
(firm, good/firm, good, good/soft, soft, heavy)

going	category	position	%	num
FIRM-	pla	6	50.00	12
FIRM-	rat	2	46.67	15
FIRM-	tra	1	40.00	10
FIRM-	ave	1	36.36	11
FIRM-	ave	2	33.33	21
FIRM-	wei	3	33.33	12
FIRM-	day	4	31.58	19
FIRM-	pla	2	30.00	10
FIRM-	ave	4	30.00	20
FIRM-	dis	1	30.00	20

going	category	position	%	num
GOOD/FIRM-	rat	1	49.30	215
GOOD/FIRM-	ave	1	40.87	345
GOOD/FIRM-	rat	2	38.07	394
GOOD/FIRM-	joc	1	36.99	438
GOOD/FIRM-	tra	1	36.25	309
GOOD/FIRM-	cou	1	35.29	221
GOOD/FIRM-	day	2	33.63	559
GOOD/FIRM-	pla	3	32.29	353
GOOD/FIRM-	ave	2	32.03	434
GOOD/FIRM-	wei	4	31.37	153

going	category	position	%	num
GOOD-	rat	1	52.37	317
GOOD-	ave	1	43.28	543
GOOD-	rat	2	34.93	607
GOOD-	joc	1	33.50	809
GOOD-	cou	1	32.94	343
GOOD-	pla	2	32.64	579
GOOD-	tra	1	31.28	745
GOOD-	ave	2	29.99	737
GOOD-	day	1	29.20	702
GOOD-	pla	3	28.55	564

going	category	position	%	num
GOOD/SOFT-	rat	1	**49.38**	160
GOOD/SOFT-	ave	1	**38.67**	256
GOOD/SOFT-	ave	2	**37.82**	312
GOOD/SOFT-	pla	2	**37.70**	252
GOOD/SOFT-	tra	1	**37.12**	264
GOOD/SOFT-	rat	2	**36.28**	317
GOOD/SOFT-	joc	1	**35.41**	353
GOOD/SOFT-	pla	3	**34.71**	242
GOOD/SOFT-	wei	4	**33.33**	141
GOOD/SOFT-	cou	1	**31.79**	151

going	category	position	%	num
SOFT-	rat	1	**52.50**	200
SOFT-	ave	1	**45.31**	320
SOFT-	joc	1	**37.98**	466
SOFT-	pla	2	**37.46**	315
SOFT-	tra	1	**37.22**	360
SOFT-	rat	2	**36.29**	350
SOFT-	rat	3	**36.08**	352
SOFT-	ave	2	**34.70**	389
SOFT-	day	1	**32.98**	470
SOFT-	dis	1	**32.14**	557

going	category	position	%	num
HEAVY-	rat	1	**56.91**	123
HEAVY-	ave	1	**48.54**	206
HEAVY-	joc	1	**37.67**	292
HEAVY-	tra	1	**37.04**	243
HEAVY-	day	1	**36.56**	279
HEAVY-	rat	2	**36.24**	218
HEAVY-	rat	3	**35.94**	217
HEAVY-	pla	2	**35.94**	192
HEAVY-	ave	2	**35.89**	248
HEAVY-	day	2	**35.71**	280

SORTING THE WHEAT FROM THE CHAFF

By now you would have realised there are a lot of tables in the preceding chapters; far too many to memorise in fact. I published them in order to cover as many bases as possible so that any reader, whatever their particular interest, can find what they may be looking for. However, that does mean there is a lot of information that will not interest everyone. In this section I have sorted all of the information into tables with relevant priorities to make it easier.

    In the following table I took all of the best profit/loss figures and put them into one table and then sorted them to show the most profit as in column 5. The first column is an extra column to denote win or each way:-

Win/ew	type	category	position	profit/loss%	num
e/w	HAW-12+	pla	6	144.13	61
win	HAW-12+	pla	6	122.00	61
e/w	HAW-12+	wei	1	119.25	121
e/w	HAW-12+	rat	6	112.13	33
e/w	HAW-12+	ave	5	106.38	73
win	HAW-12+	wei	1	105.00	121
win	HAW-4-11	rat	3	95.50	154
e/w	HAW-12+	day	5	93.50	33
win	HAW-12+	ave	5	93.00	73
win	HAW-12+	rat	6	89.00	33
win	HAW-12+	day	5	82.00	33
e/w	HAW-4-11	rat	3	76.61	154
e/w	HH-12+	pla	9	60.25	14
e/w	HFL-12+	rat	5	53.94	34
win	HFL-12+	rat	5	51.75	34
e/w	NAW-4-11	rat	4	48.33	42
e/w	NH-4-11	ave	2	47.51	89
win	NH-12+	day	4	46.14	66
win	NAW-4-11	rat	4	42.00	42
win	HH-12+	pla	9	41.00	14
e/w	HCH-12+	pla	2	40.70	45
win	NH-4-11	ave	2	38.38	89
e/w	NH-12+	day	4	37.41	66
win	HH-12+	rat	3	37.00	65
win	HFL-12+	day	1	37.00	66
e/w	HCH-12+	day	1	35.70	60
e/w	HFL-12+	pla	7	34.63	30
e/w	HAW-12+	ave	4	34.60	67
win	HAW-12+	ave	4	34.38	67
e/w	NFL-4-11	rat	3	34.30	55
win	HFL-4-11	cou	1	34.05	81
win	HFL-4-11	cou	1	34.05	81
win	HAW-12+	day	2	32.88	127
win	HFL-12+	pla	7	32.50	30
e/w	HAW-4-11	wei	4	32.14	16

In this next table I removed all the categories and positions that had less than 50 examples. The reason for this is that I believe this gives a better and more reliable statistic than examples of less than 50. In the main part of this book I have used less than 10 as the cut off point and this was because I wanted to show as much information as possible.

Only Statistics with More than 50 examples from the previous table

win/ew	type	category	position	profit/loss%	num
e/w	HAW-12+	pla	6	144.13	61
win	HAW-12+	pla	6	122.00	61
e/w	HAW-12+	wei	1	119.25	121
e/w	HAW-12+	ave	5	106.38	73
win	HAW-12+	wei	1	105.00	121
win	HAW-4-11	rat	3	95.50	154
win	HAW-12+	ave	5	93.00	73
e/w	HAW-4-11	rat	3	76.61	154
e/w	NH-4-11	ave	2	47.51	89
win	NH-12+	day	4	46.14	66
win	NH-4-11	ave	2	38.38	89
e/w	NH-12+	day	4	37.41	66
win	HH-12+	rat	3	37.00	65
win	HFL-12+	day	1	37.00	66
e/w	HCH-12+	day	1	35.70	60
e/w	HAW-12+	ave	4	34.60	67
win	HAW-12+	ave	4	34.38	67
e/w	NFL-4-11	rat	3	34.30	55
win	HFL-4-11	cou	1	34.05	81
win	HFL-4-11	cou	1	34.05	81
win	HAW-12+	day	2	32.88	127
win	HFL-12+	ave	3	32.00	50
e/w	HCH-12+	ave	2	31.76	68
win	HCH-12+	ave	2	31.50	68
e/w	HFL-4-11	cou	1	29.97	81
e/w	HFL-4-11	cou	1	29.97	81
e/w	HFL-4-11	pla	5	29.85	77
win	HFL-4-11	pla	5	29.00	77
e/w	HFL-12+	ave	3	27.63	50
win	NFL-4-11	rat	3	26.80	55
win	HAW-4-11	ave	5	24.74	87
e/w	NH-4-11	tra	1	23.62	88
e/w	NH-4-11	tra	1	23.62	88
win	HFL-12+	wei	2	22.50	111
plac	HAW-12+	pla	6	22.13	61

The problem with the previous table is that it includes a lot of categories/positions that are not easy to assimilate from the newspaper. For example- HAW-12+ in the fourth row gives ave 5 as showing a profit of £106.38 but, it takes a bit of doing to calculate which horses in a HAW race of 12+ runners that have the fifth best average from the last three form figures. Not impossible mind you and it depends how much work you want to do but, I guess a lot of people would not want to do this. So, in the next table I removed all of the categories/positions from the previous table except pla 1, 2 and 3 – ave 1, 2 and 3 – rat 1,2and 3 and c&d. I have included c&d as there are not usually that many course and distance winners in a race. These categories/positions are not too difficult to work out and assimilate from a newspaper.

Only with places, averages, ratings 1, 2, 3 and course & distance winners

win/ew	type	category	position	profit/loss%	num
win	HAW-4-11	rat	3	95.50	154
e/w	HAW-4-11	rat	3	76.61	154
e/w	NH-4-11	ave	2	47.51	89
win	NH-4-11	ave	2	38.38	89
win	HH-12+	rat	3	37.00	65
e/w	NFL-4-11	rat	3	34.30	55
win	HFL-12+	ave	3	32.00	50
e/w	HCH-12+	ave	2	31.76	68
win	HCH-12+	ave	2	31.50	68
e/w	HFL-12+	ave	3	27.63	50
win	NFL-4-11	rat	3	26.80	55
e/w	HAW-12+	pla	1	21.44	60
e/w	NH-4-11	pla	2	21.20	86
win	NH-4-11	pla	2	20.54	86
e/w	HH-12+	rat	3	20.00	65
win	HFL-4-11	c&d	1	16.30	63
win	HAW-12+	c&d	1	15.13	121
plac	HH-4-11	ave	2	10.48	114
plac	HH-12+	rat	2	9.91	70
plac	NH-4-11	ave	2	9.13	89
plac	NFL-4-11	pla	2	8.35	67
plac	HAW-12+	pla	1	8.19	60
plac	NFL-4-11	rat	3	7.50	55
win	NH-12+	joc	1	7.19	76
plac	NAW-4-11	ave	2	5.98	57
plac	NH-12+	pla	2	4.80	62
e/w	HFL-4-11	c&d	1	-2.94	63
e/w	HAW-12+	c&d	1	-3.03	121
win	HCH-4-11	c&d	1	-5.13	68
e/w	HCH-4-11	c&d	1	-6.27	68
win	HAW-4-11	c&d	1	-69.00	193
e/w	HAW-4-11	c&d	1	-100.59	193

I realised that not all people buy a daily newspaper and the criteria used for rating horses may vary in different publications. Many people rely on the papers provided by the bookmakers themselves. So the following table is taken from the previous one but, without the results for ratings (rat).

From the previous table but, without rating (rat)

win/ew	type	category	position	profit/loss%	num
e/w	NH-4-11	ave	2	47.51	89
win	NH-4-11	ave	2	38.38	89
win	HFL-12+	ave	3	32.00	50
e/w	HCH-12+	ave	2	31.76	68
win	HCH-12+	ave	2	31.50	68
e/w	HFL-12+	ave	3	27.63	50
e/w	HAW-12+	pla	1	21.44	60
e/w	NH-4-11	pla	2	21.20	86
win	NH-4-11	pla	2	20.54	86
win	HFL-4-11	c&d	1	16.30	63
win	HAW-12+	c&d	1	15.13	121
plac	HH-4-11	ave	2	10.48	114
plac	NH-4-11	ave	2	9.13	89
plac	NFL-4-11	pla	2	8.35	67
plac	HAW-12+	pla	1	8.19	60
win	NH-12+	joc	1	7.19	76
plac	NAW-4-11	ave	2	5.98	57
plac	NH-12+	pla	2	4.80	62
e/w	HFL-4-11	c&d	1	-2.94	63
e/w	HAW-12+	c&d	1	-3.03	121
win	HCH-4-11	c&d	1	-5.13	68
e/w	HCH-4-11	c&d	1	-6.27	68
win	HAW-4-11	c&d	1	-69.00	193
e/w	HAW-4-11	c&d	1	-100.59	193

LAST WORD

When I started this book I considered it my job to set out these statistics clearly and honestly. To show as much information as possible and the best information without making the book too large and thereby cumbersome. Also, I wanted to keep down the cost of publishing and therefore the cost to you. This was an important consideration and I hope I have achieved these objectives and I have produced an honest concise book that is not too expensive.

The information has taken a long time to collect and quite a lot of time and effort has been used in devising the programs and sorting that information. Therefore, I hope you find the book informative, good value and a good reference guide. I guess it will be mainly people who use horse racing as a gambling medium who will buy the book but, I believe there is something of interest for anyone involved in horse racing.

Most gamblers like to do their own thing and follow their own strategies and I believe the information and statistics in this book will assist in that objective. My purpose of this book was not to provide any advice into how people should gamble or follow any particular strategy. This left me to be impartial and just provide the statistics as I found them without any influence on my part. In the end analysis I felt this was the best thing to do.

I hope you enjoy the book and find it helpful in whatever strategy you use.

Good luck in all of your endeavours.

Mark Gaster

Also by this author.

"COARSE FISHING – THE BEST WAY"

A statistical analysis of the conditions of month, wind speed, wind direction, weather, air temperatures, water temperatures, barometric pressure, water colour and moon phase in relation to coarse fishing.

LISTED online at

WH SMITH
AMAZON
WATERSTONES

INDEX

Printed in Great Britain
by Amazon.co.uk, Ltd.,
Marston Gate.